Seeing Earth:

Literary Responses to Space Exploration

Seeing Earth:

Literary Responses to Space Exploration

Ronald Weber

Ohio University Press
Athens, Ohio   London

Library of Congress Cataloging in Publication Data

Weber, Ronald, 1934-
  Seeing earth.

  Bibliography: p.
  Includes index.
  1. American literature—20th century—History and criticism.
2. Outer space in literature. 3. Space flight in literature.
4. Earth in literature. 5. Astronautics in literature. 6. Astronauts in literature. 7. Outer space—Exploration—United
States—History. I. Title.
PS228.096W43   1984   810'.9356   84-16567
ISBN 0-8214-0791-0

For Elizabeth, Andrea, and Kathryn

Contents

The earth—that is sufficient;
I do not want the constellations any nearer;
I know they are very well where they are;
I know they suffice for those who belong to them.

Walt Whitman: "Song of the Open Road"

Preface

I missed *Apollo 11*. While Aldrin and Armstrong walked on the moon I was on a ship crossing the Atlantic, returning from a Fulbright year in Europe. The few details that came over the ship's radio were relayed to the passengers, but I missed the experience of watching the historic moon landing on live television. What I remember most about *Apollo 11* is a conversation in a Chock Full O'Nuts in New York one rainy afternoon soon after my ship docked. Next to me on a counter stool was a grizzled skid-row type. He sized me up and said, "You know why we got all this rain?"

I admitted I didn't.

"It's because of the rocks them astronauts took off the moon." He pointed a finger skyward, emphasizing the point. "And it won't get no better till they put 'em back."

A few years later I spent several months in Florida near Cape Canaveral. I went on tours of the launch facilities and attended a space congress in Cocoa Beach where some of the astronauts spoke. But what I remember most about that period is the launch of a communications satellite with an Atlas-Centaur rocket, small in comparison with the rockets that sent men to the moon. The launch was at night, and from the vantage point of Jetty Park the sight was dazzling. The rocket rose slowly, a tube of orange fire that colored the entire sky. Higher, the fire turned silver-white and the rocket arced over in the sky and finally disappeared into the stars. The crowd, sitting on blankets and atop cars, cheered the rocket's flight. Afterwards, they stayed on, talking, drinking beer, like people at a fireworks display who refuse to believe the show is really over.

My latest brush with the space program came just before the launch of the first space shuttle. I was on a sailing trip, the boat leaving from Port Canaveral and headed into the Atlantic along the Cape. It was a fine day and we decided to sail far out for a glimpse of the shuttle on its launch pad. I remember that it was much larger than I expected, a blocky arrow aimed to the sky, shimmering white in the sun. I remember something else as well. I was trailing a fishing line, as I'm inclined to do on lazy sailing days, and just as I was gazing across the water at the shuttle a fish struck. It seemed as if I had the fish for several minutes, but it was probably only a second or so before the line broke and I was left with the peculiarly empty feeling of clutching a lifeless rod, the monofilament fluttering in the breeze.

Looking back, there seems to be a link of sorts between my few experiences with the space program and the views examined in the following pages. My thoughts about the great achievements of American space exploration and the promise of a space-centered future are intertwined with recollections of a conversation about moon rocks and rain, of a mild evening in a park after the sky had turned orange, of a fish that got away. I try to give space exploration its full due; it is, I am sure, one of the most enduring achievements of our age. But I cannot quite separate it from my homely memories. The space shuttle keeps bringing me back to a lost fish. When the first shuttle left the earth on its flawless flight I cheered—and wondered about a fish somewhere off the Cape with a hook embedded in its jaw.

My interest in the literature of space exploration grows out of an interest in the theme of the journey in American culture. The culture had its origins in the journey of Europeans to a new world, and for most of our history the excursions into and across America comprised the essential drama of the culture. Journeys, real and imagined, have in turn provided us with some of our most characteristic books, from Alexis de Tocqueville's *Democracy in America* (drawn from a journey through Jacksonian America recently retraced in Richard Reeves's *American Journey*) to Mark Twain's *The Adventures of Huckleberry Finn*, from *The Journals of Lewis and Clark* to Jack Kerouac's *On the Road*. With the culture settled into a comfortable middle age, we journey less—or find fewer destinations for our travels that are not simply mirrors of our familiar departure points—yet those literary explorers lingering among us still touch a responsive chord, as witness the recent interest in John McPhee's venture into Alaska in *Coming into the Country* or Jonathan Raban's chronicle of motoring down the Mississippi River in *Old Glory: An American Voyage* or William Least Heat Moon's account of criss-crossing America in *Blue Highways*.

But however much our appetite for the journey remains, there is now the unavoidable sense that we are only retracing our steps, rediscovering what has long been discovered. John Seelye has noted that in the beginning "America was, more than anything, space," a *tabula rasa* for acting out and imagining out dreams of radical transformation. We can hardly now escape the fact that our space has been largely filled in with the embodiments, tawdry and grand, of those dreams. In our post-frontier restlessness we have sought fresh adventures. We have looked out at the rest of the world and imagined it as blank space, emptiness, to be molded in one way or another to visions of political and economic truth. And we have looked beyond the world into true space, outer space, and launched yet another national journey.

It is the literary embodiment of this newest and perhaps ultimate phase of American journeying, the journey into outer space, that is the subject of this book. I first began looking at this material to see to what extent, if any, it drew on the motifs and metaphors of our earlier journeys. Were there parallels between, for example, the literary treatments of the westward movement and the journey to the moon? Were they portrayed as different historical expressions of a common national thrust into a regenerative unknown? *Apollo 8* astronaut William Anders suggested such a link between space and the exploration of the West when he remarked that the "Appalachian Trail, the wide Missouri . . . they were there, and men came to conquer them and to benefit from them. Now space was our frontier, and here I was in the lead wagon." Or were the moon flights simply an expression of a technological America, spurred on by Cold War rivalry, that bore no relation to cultural themes? Lewis Mumford thought that with the *Apollo 11* moon landing "the frontier is closed" and that the traditional American exploring spirit was reduced to blind technological advancement. "The landing of the first two astronauts on the moon," he wrote, "was not the beginning of a new age of cosmic exploration but the end. The scientific technological revolution that began in the sixteenth century therewith reached its appropriately sterile terminus: a satellite as uninhabitable as the earth itself will all too soon become."

I have come to believe that it is still too early in the age of space to begin to answer such questions. After the moon-orbiting flight of *Apollo 8* the *New York Times* remarked in an editorial that "man is still too close to this staggering crossing of the space frontier to grasp the full significance of what has been accomplished." That still seems to me the case. In manned space exploration we have not yet ventured far from earth, and the men who have done the venturing—and told us what it was like— have so far been a narrow breed of courageous experts.

Our space technology, as Walter A. McDougall has noted, remains only at the stage of maturity achieved by the railroads in the 1860s or radio in the 1920s. Perhaps not until our commitment to space exploration is much greater than it now is and men (as Norman Mailer remarks later in these pages) who speak like Shakespeare ride the rockets will we have sufficient material, and sufficient perspective on it, to see our space journeys in light of the deepest cultural themes. But even then it may be difficult for us to measure space exploration in light of the journeys of the past. Unlike earlier explorers, the explorers of space will remain removed from the worlds they traverse, encapsulated in space suits and space vehicles, supported by a human pyramid of earth-bound technicians; their struggles will be with mechanical malfunctions rather than hostile environments; the stories they tell will likely be of technical achievements more than human striving. Indeed, as Richard S. Lewis has pointed out, the story of every space mission, pre-written into a flight plan, is known in advance, with the result that space exploration is—and is likely to remain—one of the most regimented of human activities. Catastrophe is the only surprise.

This book attempts only a brief survey of American writing about space exploration—and it calls attention to a dominant use of space exploration in this work as a means of deflecting attention back to earth and earthly concerns. It is offered as a preliminary report, the first of its kind, and one that no doubt will require considerable adjustment and amplification if the exploration of space continues and we enter deeply into the space age. The first chapter introduces the subject, separates the literary response to space exploration into two broad categories, and offers some possible explanations for the importance of earth in accounts of space. The second chapter examines the treatment of space exploration in the work of scholarly writers, including sociologists, historians, philosophers, and theologians. The third chapter turns to books written by the men who have traveled in space, the astronauts, and in one case to a book by an astronaut who abandoned the program. The next three chapters examine, in turn, the uses of space exploration in the work of novelists, poets, and those journalists who have written about space at book length. The seventh and final chapter again draws attention to the lure of earth in our accounts of space, a preference for what Neil Armstrong, standing in the Sea of Tranquillity, thought of as the "remote blue planet" as against, in the words of his fellow moon-walker "Buzz" Aldrin, the "magnificent desolation" of the lunar landscape—a preference that stands (for the moment, at least) as our most characteristic literary response to space. In the reference section I list, by chapter and alphabetically by author, the sources of quotations and references in the text.

Portions of the study, in altered form, have appeared as articles in *Exploration, The Georgia Review, The Journal of Popular Culture*, and *Notre Dame Magazine.* Part of chapter six appeared in an appendix to my book, *The Literature of Fact: Literary Nonfiction in American Writing* (Athens, Ohio: Ohio University Press, 1980). I am grateful for permission to draw upon this material. Work on the study was aided by a summer grant from the College of Arts and Letters, University of Notre Dame.

1 Great-Circle Sailing

"So I suppose we must jump off," Mr. Sammler decides, "because it is our human fate to do so." The prospect of man heading for the stars does not fill the aged hero of Saul Bellow's novel with anticipation; his planet, *Mr. Sammler's Planet*, is still the earth, and personally he has no desire to go to Europe let alone the moon. Moreover, he believes that if it were purely a rational matter we would establish justice here before leaving for other worlds. But Sammler recognizes in mankind a compulsion to do what can be done—and in the latter part of the twentieth century that means journeying into space.

Bellow's 1970 novel is filled with speculation on space travel and the colonization of the moon. One of the characters tells Sammler that he has already made a reservation with Pan American for a future moon flight, the 512th person to sign up. Since the novel's publication the age of space travel, and perhaps space colonization, has come even closer. The space shuttle system makes it possible, at least in theory, for people without special training to venture into space. Abundant time and money have been devoted to considering what they might do there (inhabit orbiting space stations, engage in manufacturing, pursue scientific research), and this potential activity has been popularized in such books as Gerald O'Neill's *The High Frontier* (1977), Stewart Brand's *Space Colonies* (1977), and Nigel Calder's *Spaceships of the Mind* (1978).

But since manned missions in space are considerably

more expensive than comparable unmanned missions (roughly fifty to one-hundred times more expensive), the immediate future may well see more machine than human efforts in space. Except for military purposes, additional moon missions of any sort seem unlikely. In a *New York Times* article on the tenth anniversary of the *Apollo 11* moon landing, Tom Wolfe remarked that it was evident that "the moon was in economic terms pretty much what it looked like from Earth, a gray rock." He added that the few technological spinoffs from the moon program hardly amounted to a giant step for mankind. As for deep space, the immense distances have caused some observers to believe there will be relatively few space missions and little if any colonization. C. P. Snow could envision future research stations in the solar system, but beyond this he thought that the distances of the universe "will defeat us, in all human probability, forever." He recalled Pascal's remark that the silence of the infinite spaces frightened him, and added: "It is the spaces themselves which frighten me." The physicist Freeman Dyson, on the other hand, has pictured a coming "romantic age" in space flight that will be dominated by multitudes of inexpensive solar sailboats winging their way through immense emptiness. Similarly, James E. Oberg, in this study of the Russian space program, *Red Star in Orbit* (1981), envisions a dozen Soviet space outposts by the end of the century that will be inhabited by people ("a few hundred") who will produce children in space and think of themselves as permanent space settlers.

Whatever may lie ahead in space activity, it is evident to some that we are already entered upon what Carl Sagan has called "a golden age of planetary exploration." Whether we make use of it or not, we have at our disposal the capacity to extend the human presence beyond the earth—and with it the opportunity to view ourselves in a radically different manner. We no longer need see ourselves, in Sagan's words, as "restricted to a single world" but as inhabitants of the solar system and possessed of a solar-system consciousness. Interviewed on television during the *Apollo 11* moon landing, Ray Bradbury went further. The whole point of space exploration, he said, was man's effort "to relate himself to the total universe," to "be at home in the universe."

Whether such an enlargement of human consciousness takes place of course remains to be seen. All that is certain is that over the past quarter century remarkable things have been accomplished in space. Men traveled to the moon and walked upon it; man's machines soared far beyond our nearest star; man's imagination searched through the solar system, pursuing signs of life on distant bodies that seemed to bear some resemblance to earth. It is unlikely that the adventure in space will end with these deeds. If it is true, as James Michener remarked, that the "specific challenge of our age" is the exploration of space, we may have little choice but to forge ahead. Michener added: "Space is indifferent to what we do; it has no feeling, no design, no interest in whether we grapple with it or not. But we cannot be indifferent to space, because the grand slow march of our intelligence has brought us, in our generation, to a point from which we can explore and understand and utilize it. To turn back now would be to deny our history, our capabilities." But whether we continue with space exploration or turn back is, once again, a matter for the future.

This study does not try to imagine that future. Rather it looks back over the early years of American space exploration; in particular, it looks back at what our writers thought and felt about space exploration, at how they described and interpreted it. By writers I mean those novelists, poets, journalists, and scholars who in some manner drew on space in their work and attempted to locate it in some context of interpretation. I include in this group astronauts who gave us written accounts of their experiences in space—and I exclude journalists and historians who

only recounted what took place in space and science fiction writers who spun space adventures set in the future.
In the material it looks at, the study does not pretend to
completeness, though of course I hope the works examined accurately reflect a broad national response on the
part of writers to space exploration. I hope as well that the
study makes some contribution to the major study yet to
be written of the full impact of space upon the national
consciousness. Such a study, as Leo Marx has noted, necessarily involves the larger question of the impact of me-
chanization itself upon consciousness, a complex and
obscure subject, but one that must be clarified before we
can adequately understand our respones to the journey
into space.

Our literary responses to the space age can be separated
into two broad categories. There are those, with Sagan,
who treated space exploration as a liberating leap into a
mysterious future, an adventuresome launch onto a new
ocean, a great opening-out of the mind and spirit. "We
have put our ships into the cosmic ocean," Sagan wrote.
"The waters are benign and we have learned to sail. No
longer are we bound to our solitary island Earth." In his
popular book *Cosmos* (1980), Sagan used the same aquat-
ic language to stimulate a compelling vision of space exploration: "The surface of the Earth is the shore of the
cosmic ocean. From it we have learned most of what we
know. Recently, we have waded a little out to sea, enough
to dampen our toes or, at most, wet our ankles. The water
seems inviting. The ocean calls. Some part of our being
knows this is from where we came. We long to return."
Daniel Boorstin cast a similar view in peculiarly American terms by suggesting that space exploration was
simply the latest chapter in the long national fascination
with the unknown. Indeed, space exploration provides a
means of renewing the traditional American exploring
spirit. Boorstin wrote: "We must remember that we live in

a new world. We must keep alive the exploring spirit. We must not sacrifice the infinite promise of the unknown, of man's unfulfilled possibilities in the universe's untouched mysteries, for the cozy satisfaction of predictable, statistical beliefs. Space exploration is the symbol." After dismissing the resistance of some intellectuals to the space program, a writer for the *Wall Street Journal* declared that "moon exploration is only the beginning of the long stride across the ages of man. It is only one more way-station along man's eternal journey toward the new and unknown."

Perhaps no one was more rhapsodic in portraying the compelling forward thrust of space exploration than the dark genius of rocketry, Wernher von Braun. Neil Armstrong's step onto the surface of the moon seemed to him comparable only with the evolutionary moment when life crawled onto land. As long as man remained bound to the earth he shared in earth's eventual extinction; but with *Apollo 11*, as von Braun phrased it, that "fateful chain" was broken and man was now able to live and work elsewhere in the solar system. In freeing himself from bondage to earth, man had opened the way for the maintenance of life and thus grasped for himself the only kind of immortality within his reach. Von Braun wrote: "Immortality—not for the individual but for the species or even for the spark of life inself in our corner of the universe—nothing less than that may have been the ultimate historic meaning of those footprints on Tranquillity Base." Ray Bradbury offered the same momentous interpretation of the Apollo moon landing. He saw it as "an effort to become immortal." If man remained tied to earth he was doomed by the eventual death of the sun; only a great migration into space could save the species and preserve life. "So in order to insure the entire race existing a million years from today," Bradbury said, "a billion years from today, we're going to take our seed out into space and we're going to plant it on other worlds." In a poem, Bradbury posed the continuation of space exploration as a question, but his own answer was clear. To survive, mankind had to venture "onward to lost Mars":

> 'Which shall it be,'
> Sink back to dust and tomb, to worms and
>   grave,
> Or onward to lost Mars and mankind save?
> And star-blown winds then echo endlessly,
> Which shall it be?
> Oh wandering man, which shall, which shall
>   it be?

The other broad response to space exploration was inward turning. In this view the new feeling for earth brought about by space exploration was more compelling than eager anticipation of the plunge into the unknown; rather than freeing ourselves from bondage to earth, space exploration returned us to the planet with fresh eyes for its beauty and new appreciation of its sensual reality. "As with a childhood home," Harrison Schmitt, the last astronaut to leave the moon, remarked, "we see the earth clearly only as we prepare to leave it." Norman Cousins concluded about the *Apollo 11* moon landing that the "most significant achievement of that lunar voyage was not that man set foot on the Moon, but that he set eyes on the Earth." John Dos Passos thought, with Boorstin, that space flights rekindled the "smoldering spirit of adventure" that was "buried deep down under the routine of every day." But what stirred him most deeply was the picture of earth rising above the rim of the moon. He wrote: "The literary imagination has been pretty good in forecasting discoveries, but not all the science fiction in the paperbacks could have forecasted the astonishment, the awe, the feeling of your heart turning a somersault inside you, you felt when you first saw the photograph of the lovely living earth rising above the dead horizon of the moon."

Edwin E. "Buzz" Aldrin, the second man on the moon, captured the inward-turning response to space exploration when he called the account of his space adventure *Return to Earth* (1973) and began the book with capsule dropping into the sea rather than with the rocket launch to the moon. A children's book by Sylvia Engdahl drew on the return-to-earth theme in its title, *Our World is Earth* (1979). In the book a youngster imagines that he travels into space and meets space creatures who ask him to describe earth. The description he provides sets off the colorful, attractive earth from harsh and barren space. About the moon the child says: "I'd like to see its strange, stark beauty. But I'm not sure I'd want it to be my world." Novelists Ken Kesey and Richard Brautigan commented on space exploration in similar fashion. "A lot of people who want to get into space never got into the earth," Kesey said in response to the space colonization ideas of O'Neill's *The High Frontier*. "It's James Bond. It's turning away from the juiciness of stuff." * Brautigan remarked: "I like the planet. It's my home and I think it needs our attention and love. Let the stars wait a while longer. They are good at it."

Before the launch of *Apollo 17* in December of 1972, ending a moonlanding venture that cost some $25-billion over eleven years, John Noble Wilford of the *New York Times* asked a number of scholars to assess the Apollo program. Their responses fell into the two large categories. Arthur Schlesinger, Jr., spoke about man bursting his terrestrial bonds and pursuing the quest for knowledge and understanding that belongs to his innermost nature. Claude Levi-Strauss stressed the liberating effect of the Apollo program. "The Apollo shots open a little window" on what he called "this sad world where we live." "It is the one experience . . . the one moment when the pris-

---

*Later, with the successful space shuttle flights, Kesey appeared to change his mind. He told a *Saturday Review* writer that space was the "last new frontier" and the nation's "destiny is off the planet."

on opens on something other than the world in which we are condemned to live." Other scholars located the benefit of Apollo in the instruction it offered restless man on what he had left behind. Margaret Mead said: "We have to credit space exploration with the discovery that there is no meaningful life elsewhere in the solar system. . . . That throws more responsibility on us and on the way we live on earth, for there's nowhere else to go."

Such a divided response to space exploration, one in which it is viewed both as a liberating escape from confinement to earth and as a liberating return to fresh connection with earth, was perhaps inevitable. Victor Ferkiss opened his book *Technological Man* (1969) by recounting his first curious meeting with an astronaut. The man seemed to him a new "hero of technological civilization"; in him the "human race had found a new freedom from limitations, had crossed, however haltingly, a new threshold." Yet the banquet at which the astronaut appeared was an unchanged ritual occasion that seemed firmly entrenched in the past. And the astronaut himself and his fellow spacemen seemed conventional and even dull. Ferkiss wondered: "Could these be the supermen whom the race had struggled for a million years to produce?" The point Ferkiss wished to make through the story was the recognition that the future always arrives embedded in the past and present—or as he put it, "the new civilization will exist side by side with the old, gradually replacing it but never completely so." He went on: "The survival power of old orders—their institutions, their ideas, their ruling classes—is simply enormous. Inertia is the most important factor in human society. Man is the animal who relinquishes nothing. He simply adds to what he already is and has." The same point might be made with reference to Raymond Williams's emphasis on the simultaneous presence of residual and emergent as well as dominant elements within the dynamics of modern culture. Our responses to space exploration inevitably appealed

both to the old and the new, to the residual as well as the
emergent, to a simpler, gritty, earth-centered kind of existence (as extolled, for example, in the various *Whole Earth*
catalogs with their space photos on the covers and "tools"
described within) and at the same time to a new, exotic,
space-centered existence (as envisioned in a work like *The
High Frontier*).

But if such division was to be expected given the uneven
manner of cultural change, it nonetheless seems clear that
appeals to residual elements in human experience, to the
past and to home, were the stronger and more striking in
treatments of space exploration by writers. The new-
ocean response to space was not lacking; it had spokes-
man, like Sagan, of stirring visionary power. But the
return-to-earth theme was central in the work of writers.
In his study of Western man's changing conceptions of the
universe, *The View from Planet Earth* (1981), Vincent
Cronin locates the greatest gain in man's "world-picture"
as result of *Apollo 11* in the rediscovery of the earth. "Man
went to the moon," he observes, "but found the Earth." So
too did writers.

Several explanations come to mind for the emphasis on
earth in treatments of space exploration. Surely one is the
now conventional notion that, having seen the earth
whole from space, we have a fresh perspective on the
planet and consequently heightened concern for it. The
concern may take the form of new awareness of the fragil-
ity of the planet that leads to ecological appeals and interest in small-scale, do-it-yourself enterprises. Wendell
Berry, for example, objected to O'Neill's space colony
ideas on the grounds that they would add to big government and so increase tax burdens on those working in
craft shops and on small farms to create a more humane,
nature-centered existence on earth. It also may take the
form of a new sense of the oneness of earth that over-
whelms national boundaries and ethnic and racial differ-

ences, promoting political and social solidarity. Philip Slater summed up this response to space exploration when he wrote in his book *Earthwalk* (1974):

> Perhaps the most classic example of social eversion concerns an oft-noted by-product of the space program. Nothing could be more linear than the kind of scientific thinking that produced space exploration. It represents the extreme form of agency, of limitless narcissistic striving. Yet one major consequence of the space program is that it enabled masses of people to look back on our dwindling planet and reconceptualize it as "spaceship earth"— as a small, interdependent totality. Ecological consciousness on a mass scale thus sprang directly from the fullest expression of its precise opposite—a straight line creating its own curving.

The biophysicist John Platt made the same point when, in response to the *Times* survey before *Apollo 17*, he remarked: "That great picture of earth taken from the moon is one of the most powerful images in the minds of men today and may be worth the cost of the whole Apollo project. It is changing our relationship to the earth and to each other. I see that as a great landmark in exploration— to get away from the earth to see it whole."

Another explanation is to be found in the nature of much of the material examined in the following pages, the work of writers and scholars. In *The Machine and the Garden* (1964), Leo Marx traced the long hold on the American literary imagination of the pastoral ideal, the desire to withdraw from the complexities of civilization into a simple, natural, rural life, as well as a concomitant pessimism about the machine and technological progress. In subsequent work Marx has noted that what was once a "rarefied literary attitude" has, since World War II, been broadly extended to include a large segment of politically disaffected intellectuals, writers, teachers, students, and professionals. In part, the change was inspired by a number of events, beginning with the use of the atom bomb against Hiroshima, that caused doubt and fear about the consequences of new technological developments. Another factor was the widespread use of "technology" during the 1960s to represent the principle of authority and oppression in the country and to spur radical attitudes. Marx has pointed as well to what may be a general susceptibility to the "fatalistic idea of technology" stemming from disappointment over excessively optimistic social expectations, the machine made the scapegoat for the failure to attain the full measure of the American promise. But whatever the complete range of explanation, it was evident to Marx at the beginning of the 1980s that the national imagination was now marked by a "powerful attraction" to the "dark, fateful, well-nigh apocalyptic idea of 'technology'." For some of the writers mentioned in this study, the use of the return-to-earth theme may spring from similarly ingrained pessimistic attitudes about the role of technology in modern life and a tendency to conceive of earth, in relation to barren space, in inviting pastoral terms.* It may spring, to put it more simply, from a view of technology as a threat to life and culture rather than as an expression of life and culture.

Finally, the prevalence of the return-to-earth theme in accounts of space exploration is no doubt to some degree a manifestation of the great divorce between the scientific and literary communities. Literary intellectuals, C. P.

---

*In a 1965 discussion of "Historical Analogy: The Railroad and the Space Program and Their Impact on Society," the historian Bruce Mazlish, referring to Marx's study of the pastoral impulse in American writing, wondered whether the reverse might be true. In the work of imaginative writers would "space flights somehow take on the quality of being redemptive journeys away from society in the direction of nature?" The answer (excluding the work of science fiction writers) would seem to be no.

Snow maintained, are natural Luddites, suspicious of the claims of science and perhaps envious of its intellectual standing. In America, John Leonard has noted, writers are notoriously "hard on the case of science," and are given to portraying scientists as "evil and monsters," as "black magicians and wicked witches." As a result, writers have found themselves increasingly removed from the worlds of scientific research and technological development, at best grudging witnesses of some of the most remarkable achievements of the time. With space exploration writers have had no choice but to remain in the background, cut off from what has been the exclusive preserve of scientists and engineers. Novelists, poets, journalists, and scholars have watched from afar, removed to bleacher seats at Cape Canaveral or television sets in the living room, separated even by specialized language from active involvement in the adventure in space.*

News of the space adventure coming to writers from television and newspapers was stirring enough but oddly ephemeral. Bruce Mazlish, in a 1980 article looking back at the *Apollo 11* moon landing, noted (as many had before) how quickly interest in the achievement declined among all segments of the population. "I am puzzled," he wrote, "by the disparity between the greatness of the deed

*Artists have fared somewhat better. Early in the space program the National Aeronautics and Space Administration began inviting artists to Cape Canaveral to watch launchings. The artists were given considerable freedom to roam the launch sites and meet with astronauts and ground technicians and scientists. Robert Rauschenberg, an invited guest for the launching of *Apollo 11*, subsequently produced a much-admired series of thirty-three lithographs called *Stoned Moon*. Calvin Tomkins has said of the work that "charts and diagrams, gantry rigs, machinery, oranges, palm trees, long-necked shore birds, photos of the astronauts, images from the televised moon landings, and swarms of other details are juxtaposed in the Rauschenberg manner, with a verve and brio that lifts the series well beyond official or commemorative arts." Some artists, however, declined NASA's invitation, and one of them, Thomas Hart Benton, remarked: "I just put it out of my mind. What can I do to make a painting of a damn rocket? You'd show it better in a moving picture."

and the meanness of the result," and he turned for explanation to a number of differences between the Apollo flights and the fifteenth-century Age of Discovery: "The major difference, I believe, is that in space there are no flora and fauna. There are no people on the moon to be conquered or converted. There are no new animals to grace the parks of a Spanish king, no exotic plants to nurture in the royal gardens at Kew. . . . Space, by contrast, is 'empty,' and our chief harvest thus far has been in the form of rocks. Scientists profess delight. But there is not much to nourish the *public's* imagination."

Nor much, it would seem, to nourish the writer's imagination. Excluded from space exploration and perhaps uninspired by it as well, some writers treated the subject in their work (when they treated it at all) with bemused irony. Michael J. Arlen, writing about "The Space Race" in *The New Yorker,* imagined an escalation in a future contest with the Russians in which the U.S. reacts to a moon landing by the entire company of the Leningrad Symphony Orchestra by sending a Polaroid camera to the surface of Saturn. Arlen also wryly referred to a recent space flight that had brought back interesting data on "something that very much resembled a flight of green horseflies" encountered over Perth, Australia. J. F. Powers constructed a brief play, "Moonshot," published in *The Nation,* that drew on a news report that pumice dust on the moon might be shaped into building blocks and held together with a "waterless cement" made from sulphur. Two returned astronauts tell a Senate committee (on "Oceans, Rivers, Lakes, Harbors, and Space") about their success constructing two small buildings on the moon— and about the presence of Russian construction crews devoted to the same task. The Senators respond to the nonsense with enthusiastic talk about putting "a million men on the moon constructing buildings with pumice dust," but a "cynical reporter"—with Powers's satiric blessing—concludes: "Let me out of here!" Other writers

—and, according to Tom Wolfe, liberal intellectuals in general—responded to the space program with what Wolfe termed an "amazing hostility." Obsessed with their own cultural superiority and envious of the program's successes, they denounced it as "tasteless" and "sterile." In one way or another they conveyed the view that the scientists and engineers in the space program "may have accomplished a feat—but the feat was worthless." By the same token, scientists and engineers could appear overly protective of the venture in space, disinclined to share it with those lacking appropriate technical credentials.

One of the more unusual books to come out of the space age was Carl Sagan's *Murmurs of Earth* (1978), the story of the making of the phonograph record sent to the stars attached to the Voyager spacecraft. In the late summer of 1977, two Voyager vehicles were launched on flights to Jupiter, Uranus, and beyond; fitted to each was a gold-coated copper phonograph record meant to provide a message from the earth to any extraterrestrial civilization that might come across it. Sagan was in charge of a team that assembled the appropriate message.

If contact was made with another civilization it was clear to Sagan and his colleagues what the first communication would be about: science. It would be the one thing the two civilizations would be certain to have in common. At the base of a shared interest in science would be, in all likelihood, a common mathematics. We can imagine different forms and sources of life, Sagan remarked in the book, "but we cannot image a civilization for which one and one does not equal two or for which there is an integer interposed between eight and nine." As a result, it was decided that mathematical relationships would be a better form of interstellar communication than physics or astronomy—and because of the link between music and mathematics, music seemed the ideal material for the record. Three-quarters of the Voyager record is music, ranging from Bach, Beethoven, and Mozart to Navajo Indian chants, a Pygmy initiation song, and Louis Armstrong. The book itself is dedicated "To the makers of music—all worlds, all times." The remaining time on the record is devoted to pictures, sounds of earth, and greetings in earth's languages. What is missing from the assemblage is any hint of the world's literature.

The story of the making of the Voyager record is in book form, but man's book-making activity is not part of the story sent into space. The omission is no doubt fitting given the distancing of writers from the scientific and technological enterprise in space—together with the suspicion that book-making is a uniquely earthly activity, lacking any extraterrestrial counterpart. But there is another sense in which one might consider the omission puzzling. Sagan thought it "chancy at best" that the Voyager record (or, for that matter, the plaques earlier affixed to the Pioneer spacecraft) would reach another civilization—and perhaps even chancier that it would be deciphered if received. The only certainty was that the recorded message would reach back to the inhabitants of earth through attendant publicity and through Sagan's book.

The names of a number of American politicians were included on the record (members of the Committee on Science and Technology of the House of Representatives, for example) due to NASA pressure, causing Sagan to remark that "this part of the Voyager message is without a doubt a signal to down here rather than to up there." But this is essentially true of the record as a whole. It celebrates a sense of earthly life—and omits from the celebration a literary sensibility at odds, or at least at a remove, from the scientific mind at work in sending a spacecraft to the stars, creating a record to accompany it, and finally making a book about the record. Whatever the likely audience for the record, the audience for the book is wholly an earthly audience; but in omitting the work of writers and scholars, *Murmurs of Earth* also omits those murmurs *about* earth that have so frequently come from such figures when they have commented about space exploration. René Dubos remarked that the real importance of space activity was that it both allowed us to see for ourselves the desolation of the moon and the near planets and to experience "how colorful, warm, inviting, and diversified the earth is against the bleakness and coldness of outer space. These unique qualities originate exclusively from the activities of living things." Such a now-conventional response was neither directed into space on the Voyager record nor back to earth in the book about the record.

Yet even had writers been less removed from the world of science and able and willing to take an active role in space journeys—and been permitted to do so—their reactions to space still might have concentrated on earth more than the stars. In our literature there is a tradition that celebrates the journey as an adventure in transcendent discovery, a movement toward new places that is accompanied by the experience of a new and better self. But a contrary tradition instructs us, in Emerson's words, that the "Soul is no traveller," that travel in the deepest sense is finally circuitous and that the only true exploration is self exploration. "Our voyaging," Thoreau remarks at the end of *Walden,* "is only great-circle sailing," and T. S. Eliot concludes "Little Gidding" with a well-known formulation of the inward-turning sense of all essential journeys: "We shall not cease from exploration/ And the end of our exploring will be to arrive where we started/ And know the place for the first time." Whether they consciously drew on this latter tradition or not, those writers who commented on space exploration in the first quarter century of the space age drew attention to the origin of the rockets more than their destinations. In varied ways their work had the effect of turning us back to the place where we started, to earth and earthly life, as if they, and we, were seeing it for the first time.

2 The Last Miracle

In this book *Passages About Earth* (1974), the historian William Irwin Thompson tells about witnessing the launch of *Apollo 17* and feeling an astonishment and joy akin to religious experience. The launch suggested to him, as did the space program as a whole, that man was at last humanizing his technology, placing it side by side with a recognition of the validity of spiritual experience. For Thompson it seemed of great importance that the space flights were manned; he refers to the astronauts as "religious hicks" who "pricked the sky with a rocket, letting all the hot air out and all the heavenly vibrations in." He found significance in the fact that some astronauts had a "conversion experience" in space, leaving behind the role of "robot-like technician" to become "another Natty Bumppo leading civilization back to the Indians," that is, back to a primary awareness of earth and the acceptance of mystical consciousness. Thompson saw no particular reason to continue the space effort beyond the Apollo program, but he affirmed what had already been accomplished in space as an "important scaffolding" in the creation of a new culture more alert to the "vibrations of heaven."

The journalist and social commentator Henry Fairlie, writing about the unmanned Voyager mission in *The New Republic*, similarly—if more temperately—found philosophical and spiritual significance in space ventures. The startling photographs of the planets returned by Voyager had the effect of making the rarified theories of science suddenly concrete and thus humanly reassuring. Because of the photographs science no longer seemed "one great game or hoax," no longer the "sorcerer's apprentice, but again the handmaiden of our deepest longings," capable of inspiring awe and reverence. Even more, Fairlie found the photographs providing us with the means of a new and liberating cosmology, one in which the universe is understood as infinite and thus the future is seen not as fixed but wholly open. "Our world and the future are not closed," as Fairlie put it, " but are opening to us as never before. This is the new vitality for which we, our philosophy and our societies and our politics, have waited so long."

But the enthusiastic embrace of the space age by Thompson and Fairlie was hardly characteristic of the ways in which scholars and social thinkers generally responded to man's departures from earth. In a 1966 article on the reaction of humanists to space exploration, the theologian Martin Marty found that most work had followed a theme set out by a *New York Times* editorial writer after the launch of Russia's *Sputnik 1* on October 4, 1957. The writer had observed:

> The creature who descended from a tree or crawled out of a cave a few thousand years ago is now on the eve of incredible journeys. Yet it is not these journeys that chiefly matter. Will we be happier for seeing the other side of the moon or strolling among the Martian meadows of asphodel?
>
> The truth is at once more ominous, more exacting and more enchanting. The greatest adventure of all is not to go to the moon or to explore the rings of Saturn. It is, rather, to understand the heart and soul of man and to

turn away from wrath and destruction and
toward creativeness and brotherly love.*

Marty thought that when men actually were on the moon
the response of humanists might well be different, but in
the first period since *Sputnik* they clearly were most concerned, as he said, with "trying to 'understand the heart
and soul of man' back on colony Earth." A few scholars,
he noted, saw in space exploration an opportunity for revi-
talizing humanistic values on what appeared to them as
an old, crowded, bored, and increasingly dehumanized
earth. Nonetheless, the dominant response of scholars to
space was similar to that suggested by the *Times*
editorial—or similar to Barbara Ward's use of Buckmin-
ster Fuller's metaphor "spaceship earth" to call attention
to the precarious position of the planet and the need for
common earthly purpose.

Following Marty's early survey the response of scholars
to space exploration remained much the same. The note
most frequently struck in their work was cautionary; attention was more often drawn to what was left behind on
the adventure in space than to what might lie ahead; in
place of the awe, reverence, and fresh inspiration noted by
Thompson and Fairlie, there were often troubled second
thoughts and expressions of loss. In the work of scholars,
in other words, there was the suggestion that if a new cosmology was forced upon us by space exploration, it would
be one that prompted us to cling more tenaciously to
earth, to value all the more our lonely life in infinite space.
"Our planet," Barbara Ward remarked in *Spaceship
Earth* (1966), "is not much more than the capsule within

*The editorial appeared on October 7, 1957. The day before, the
Times editorialized in a quite different vein, calling attention to the
complete break from earth made possible by the Russian satellite: "The
sphere which now revolves in the heavens above us is the guarantee that
man can soon break completely the fetters of gravity which have hith-
erto bound life to this tiny planet. The long road to the stars is now
open."

which we have to live as human beings if we are to survive the vast space voyage upon which we have been engaged for hundreds of millennia. . . . This space voyage is totally precarious. . . . Rational behavior is the condition of survival."

At the beginning of the space age Hannah Arendt drew on the implications of space exploration in a work she described as a reconsideration of the human condition in light of the modern situation. She opened *The Human Condition* (1958) with a reference to the launching of the Russian *Sputnik* the year before, an event that seemed to her "second in importance to no other, not even to the splitting of the atom." One of the strongest responses to the launch, she noted, was a sense of relief in that man had now taken the first step in escaping from the confinement of earth. She found the response extraordinary, causing her to wonder if the final outcome of the secularization of the modern age would be the "repudiation of an Earth who was the Mother of all living creatures under the sky."

Arendt saw a link between the exploration of outer space and various modern scientific endeavors that render life more artificial and increasingly separate us from a natural existence. Like space exploration, these efforts embody a desire to escape from the imprisonment of earth and ultimately from the human condition itself. They join in what she called a broad "rebellion against human existence as it has been given, a free gift from nowhere (secularly speaking)," and seek to replace it with what man has made for himself. The result is that "though we live now, and probably always will, under the earth's conditions, we are not mere earth-bound creatures."

This revolt—or this liberation—from bondage to earth derives from the mind of modern astrophysics and its capacity to envision earthly life from an Archimedean point outside earth. Although we remain bound to earth through the human condition, we are able to act upon earth from outside it. This achievement was made possible through a breakdown of old distinctions between earth and sky and the creation of a universe mentality that, as Arendt remarks, sees nothing in earthly nature as a mere earthly happening. As mental effort, this is an astonishing achievement—an intellectual leap of the highest order. But it is also an effort that often seems to threaten what Arendt calls "the natural life process" or "nature's household."

In "Man's Conquest of Space," an article published in 1963, Arendt returned to a similar concern with the relation of space exploration to the human condition. "Has man's conquest of space," she asked, "increased or diminished his stature?" It was a question she addressed to laymen rather than scientists; her perspective was not that of the scientist's concern with physical reality but the humanist's concern with man. It was a question, she acknowledged, that made little or no sense in light of the emancipation of modern science from an anthropocentric world and ordinary sense experience; it was only through a power of imagination and abstraction that removed the mind from earth and allowed it to consider earth from some point in the universe that the pathway was opened to the moon landings. But that the question lacked relevance from the standpoint of science was not an argument against it. Arendt noted that for the scientist himself, living a good portion of his life as a citizen and in the world of ordinary sense experience, the question was a genuine one, though one that could be answered only through debate rather than empirical evidence.

As she did in *The Human Condition*, Arendt describes the modern scientific enterprise as beginning with the Archimedean effort to view earth from the vantage point of space—to conceive of oneself as Einstein's observer who is poised freely in space. But following in the wake of this majestic imaginative effort have been a horde of space scientists who have turned elegant theories into practical projects in the exploration of space, projects that in turn convincingly demonstrate the accuracy of the theories. For this purpose alone it would be enough to send unmanned machines into space; but the actual "conquest" of space requires that men themselves go where until then only human imagination had gone.

Arendt makes clear that she does not resist this effort. All the common arguments raised against space exploration—that it is too costly or the money could better be spent on earthly problems—seem to her out of tune with the magnitude of the enterprise. More importantly, she observes that the "integrity" of science is at stake in space exploration in that it requires that both utilitarian questions as well as reflections on the stature of man be left in abeyance. The fact is that all advances in science "almost automatically" result in a decrease in man's stature in that the scientist, in his role as scientist, cannot care about such matters. "The simple fact that physicists split the atom without any hesitations the very moment they knew how to do it," Arendt writes, "although they realized full well the enormous destructive potentialities of their operation, demonstrates that the scientist *qua* scientist does not even care about the survival of the human race on earth or, for that matter, about the survival of the planet itself." Consequently, Arendt saw the effort in space exploration to actually reach the Archimedean point in relation to earth as "far from being a harmless or unequivocally triumphant enterprise." It might lead us to "look down" on earthly activities, to see human activity as mere biological activity, and therefore to sharply reduce man's stature—indeed, to eliminate altogether the humanist's conception of man as the highest being known to us. She concluded: "The conquest of space and the science that made it possible have come perilously close to this point. If they ever should reach it in earnest, the stature of man would not simply be lowered by all standards we know of, it would have been destroyed."

Arendt's sense of space exploration as embodying an escape from the human condition, a turning away from it, drew a sharp denial from Bruce Mazlish. The journeys in space, he maintained, "*are* the human condition" in that they make possible a constantly enlarging, more universal habitat for man and consequently an enlarged conception of what man is and can be. Mazlish held that the significance of space ventures "is not really in terms of what they will achieve externally but what they mean for man's achieving of his internal development." In his resistance to Arendt, Mazlish portrayed space exploration as simply another step in the onward journey in search of human potential, a natural development in the evolutionary quest of man's outer adaption and inner resources. This was a view shared in its general outlines with commentators like Thompson and Fairlie, but it was a view less frequently encountered than Arendt's sense of space exploration as a threat to the human condition. Writing after the *Apollo 11* moon landing, the Italian novelist Alberto Moravia remarked that "one does not travel, survive, or dwell in space without surrendering one's humanity." Most scholars, in one manner or another, seemed to agree.

The most common form of resistance to space exploration was to argue, as the sociologist Amitai Etzioni did in a book called *The Moon-Doggle* (1964), that it had acted as a drag on the national economy and deflected attention from earthly problems. Etzioni did not wish space exploration ended, but he wanted it divorced from special-interest politics and mindless Cold-War rivalry with Russia (as did Edwin Diamond in a parallel 1964 study, *The Rise and Fall of the Space Age*). He thought its budget should be scaled down in favor of investments in schools, medical care, and the environment. He held that there was no genuine national prestige gained from technological exploits in space; real prestige depended on what could be accomplished on earth in areas of social justice and political freedom.

In a final chapter called "Facing the Earth," Etzioni maintained that the most insidious appeal of space exploration was to the spiritual benefit it supposedly offered. In his view earth provided spiritual challenge enough for man. Moreover, no discoveries in outer space seemed likely to alter our Copernican sense of man's place in the universe, nor were they likely to provide us with new metaphysical insights. If space exploration had an effect on the human spirit it was more apt to be found in the impetus it offered to materialism and the worship of technology. What was needed, both for man's social and spiritual well being, was fresh attention to earth, the only planet available for human habitation. "As we move deeper into space, we should be facing the earth," Etzioni concluded, "and allow our deprived world to set the pace. The moon must continue to be our satellite."

Other scholars also directed attention to the spiritual implications of space exploration. Paul Tillich saw space exploration as an inevitable development of human potential but pointed to possible "spiritual dangers." He wondered if it might, with the capacity it provided for looking at earth from afar, cause a final estrangement between man and the planet, with earth losing its "motherly" or nurturing character and being seen simply as a calculable object. The long process of demythologizing earth seemed as if it might be brought to a radical conclusion by space exploration. Tillich also was concerned about the impetus space exploration gave to the drive of technological civilization to thrust ahead with little concrete focus. "Of course," he remarked, "one could call the desire to learn more about cosmic space and about astronomical bodies in it, a concrete aim. But this is only an accidental aspect. The desire to go ahead whatever may be encountered gives the real impetus." The effect of this sur-

render to what Tillich called "forwardism" led ultimately
to complete emptiness—and he wondered if space exploration might not "pronounce the last word in this
respect."

Joseph Campbell found spiritual challenge rather than
danger in space exploration—challenge that he pronounced liberating. In his view, as reported in an article
by Eugene Kennedy, space exploration demands that we
change ideas about ourselves that were formulated when
we assumed earth was the center of the universe. Although
the Copernican revolution took place over four centuries
ago, for most of us it has remained a theoretical matter;
only when men stood on the moon and through television
we were able to see earth rise above the rim of the moon
was the Copernican world truly forced upon human consciousness. Before that, Campbell says, it was simply an
"invisible idea and we could go on thinking, as we did,
about an earth down here and a heaven up there." The
space age forces us to abandon such division and all similar divisions between body and soul, nature and super-
nature, flesh and spirit. Campbell explained: "With our
view of earthrise, we could see that the earth and the heavens were no longer divided but that the earth is in the
heavens. There is no division and all the theological no-
tions based on the distinction between the heavens and the
earth collapse with that realization. There is a unity in the
universe and a unity in our own experience. We can no
longer look for a spiritual order outside our own existence." The new awareness of unity has left us, in Campbell's view, with an entirely new and fluid religious sensibility. Since there are no horizons in space there ought to
be none in human experience; space exploration thrusts
us toward a spiritual "free fall into a future that is mysterious," an awareness that we "live in the stars."

For Campbell, such a shift in consciousness is all to the
good, a decisive advance in spiritual awareness. But he
noted that the religious implications of the space age are

frightening for many people, causing them to turn back to old ideas, firmer footing. One of the curious effects of the space age, then, has been to stimulate a retreat to the old, the familiar, the orthodox. An aspect of the retreat can be found in the popular interest in unidentified flying objects and visitations from outer space, interests which Campbell located in an outmoded view of deliverance coming from some power "out there." But the space age instructs us in the meaninglessness of such hope. There is no "out there"; the kingdom of God is exactly within us. Thus Campbell remarks that "the voyages into outer space turn us back to inner space," to the realization that we alone determine our fate, create our own future—a future that is experienced as a free fall into mystery. Yet if this is the new spiritual consciousness demanded by the space age, it is not that which Campbell finds unfortunately common in the present day. Rather than taking the leap into mystery, Campbell acknowledges that many believers have turned away from the radical spiritual implications of the space age in favor of the comforting presence of familiar earthly ideas. They persist in thinking about a heaven above and an earth below. Their religious sensibility remains rooted in old assumptions, old teachings.*

John Updike's fictional character Harry "Rabbit" Angstrom, a man frequently "bothered by God," would seem to provide a case in point. In *Rabbit, Run* (1960), Harry looks down at his city from a mountain height and reflects that "it seems plain, standing here, that if there is this floor there is a ceiling, that the true space in which we live is upward space." Two decades later in Updike's third

---

*A brief discussion of the effects of space exploration on fundamentalist religious belief in Raymond A. Bauer's *Second-Order Consequences: A Methodological Essay on the Impact of Technology* (1969) comes to no conclusion other than that "people have had to cope in some way with a new problem."

novel about him, *Rabbit is Rich* (1981), Harry eagerly inspects the latest news about space for what it might reveal
about his traditional belief in "upward space," in a God
in the heavens above with man on the earth below. "He is
interested in space," Updike writes about him, "and scans
the paper every day for more words on these titanic qua-
sars on the edge of everything, and in the Sunday section
studies the new up-close photos of Jupiter, expecting to
spot a clue that all those scientists have missed; God might
have a few words to say yet." For Harry Angstrom and no
doubt many others in the age of space, God still reigns
above and religious attitudes remain fixed—or, as W. H.
Auden remarked in his poem "Moon Landing," "Un-
smudged, thank God, my Moon still queens the Heavens."

In "Man's Conquest of Space," Hannah Arendt remarks that in an increasingly technological world it is
rare that man encounters anything that is not man-made
and consequently "himself in another disguise." The astronaut in space, locked into an ingenious capsule that
maintains life in a hostile environment, carries this modern tendency to an extreme. The farther he ventures from
earth the more dependent he is on earth's machines and so
becomes, in Arendt's words, "the less likely ever to meet
anything but himself."

A similar view is at the core of the strident criticism of
space exploration set out by Lewis Mumford. In *The
Myth of the Machine: The Pentagon of Power* (1970),
Mumford printed a photo of an astronaut encased in a
space suit and helmet and observed that he was a figure
totally dependent on the machine age, a man incapable
while in space of an existence free of the machine domi-
nance of the modern age. The astronaut was engaged in a
"life-denying ritual," limited to minimal bodily and mental functions that reminded Mumford of the physical
abasement sought out by early Christian monks. The

hardships accepted by the astronauts differed only in that they were in the service of technological power, or, as Mumford put it, "man's de-natured command of nature."

Rather than enlarging human existence for the astronaut, space travel narrowed it. Mumford wrote: "Humanly speaking, space technics offer a new type of nonexistence: that of the fastest possible locomotion in a uniform environment, under uniform conditions, to an equally undistinguishable uniform destination." The only benefit Mumford could detect in space exploration was an unplanned one: "a full view of the beautiful planet we live on, an inviting home for man and for all forms of life," the gift of "an organic world picture" made possible by a view of earth from the moon. The moon landings themselves offered no new age of exploration but rather the end of exploration in the sense that man had left an earth made increasingly uninhabitable by runaway technology for what was simply an uninhabitable satellite.

In *The Invisible Pyramid* (1970), Loren Eiseley develops a parallel conception of space exploration, one set, like Mumford's, against a portrait of technological civilization out of control and turned blindly to the pursuit of the future. Eiseley speaks of the "world eaters," the despoilers of earth, now loosing their "spores" into space; having spread blight through the "green world that created him," man inevitably ventures into space, there perhaps to "wreck the last disaster." But rather than dwelling on this disaster, Eiseley examines another possibility, what he calls "the last miracle."

Like Mumford's organic world picture obtained from the moon, the last miracle involves an imaginative return to earth, a return at the very "doorway to the stars" to a fresh realization that man "lies under the spell of a greater and a green enchantment which, try as he will, he can never avoid, however far he travels. The spell has been laid on him since the beginning of time—the spell of the natural world from which he sprang." What is required of

modern man, Eiseley suggests, is that he "pursue the paradox of return"—that is, as he crosses into the realm of
space he at the same time "turn and contemplate with renewed intensity the world of the sunflower forest." Of one
thing at least space exploration has instructed us clearly:
earth is a unique possession, an "incredibly precious
planetary jewel" that alone nourishes intelligent life.
Man must re-enter this world at the very moment that he
ventures to the stars; he must re-enter and preserve the
original natural world from which he sprang on his journey to civilization and eventually beyond earth. Man
must, in other words, "seek his own way home."

Eiseley takes note in the closing lines of his book not of
the triumphant moon landing of *Apollo 11* but of the
perilous journey of the damaged *Apollo 13* back to earth.
The journey evokes the "miracle" Eiseley calls for, the
miracle of a new love for earth in place of the continued
devastation that spurs us to abandon the planet. He
writes: "Man was born and took shape among earth's leafy
shadows. The most poignant thing the astronauts had revealed in their extremity was the nostalgic call still faintly
ringing on the winds from the sunflower forest."

The paradox Eiseley notes—renewed love of earth
springing from the journeys beyond earth—appears again
in William Barrett's reflections on the meaning of space
exploration in his book *Time of Need: Forms of Imagination in the Twentieth Century* (1972). Barrett tells of two
films that summed up for him the contemporary situation
in the age of space, one a documentary about the primitive
people of New Guinea, the other Stanley Kubrick's *2001:
A Space Odyssey*. The documentary dealt with archaic
man still tied to a small portion of earth and engaged in
mystical rituals, whereas *2001* dealt with advanced scientific man launched on a voyage to a remote planet. For
Barrett, Kubrick's film portrayed space as it is, bland and
anonymous; appropriately, there is a Howard Johnson's
on a satellite station above earth, suggesting that when

space is finally colonized it will become "Howard Johnson's in the sky," a synthetic, mass-produced world in
which man discovers only his own creations.

Already the facts of space exploration indicated to Barrett that space offered nothing new for man but simply
repetition of the familiar. The significance of the first
moon landing, he declares, "was answered by the third
voyage, when people were already bored by the whole routine." He went on: "The extension of ourselves into outer
space, as Kubrick shows, is only more of the same, and can
hardly tell us much about our own meaning. Time and
again we are given shots of the long cylinder of the ship
sliding through empty space until in our boredom at the
repetitive image we begin to find space itself very boring.
To try to measure man's significance against the vastness
of space leaves us only with the thought of the insignificance of vast space." Barrett's preference is for the image of
man in the documentary film. Archaic man is closer to us
and more understandable than the programmed space
man of the future; art and religion still matter in his life,
whereas for space man they are merely diversions within
the monotony of space voyages or aspects of "emotional
engineering" used to soothe human feelings. Genuine art,
Barrett observes, is a "product of the archaic past of our
nature" and remains vital only as long as we retain some
tie to that past.

In the book's epilogue Barrett points out that our present capacity to leave earth behind in favor of space coin-
cides with the rapid disappearance of archaic man around
the globe. Does this mean, he wonders, that man has left a
primitive stage of his development forever behind him?
The answer, he believes, is no. Beneath the surface of
modern consciousness we retain a tie with archaic man;
while our knowledge enables us to leave earth, another
part of us reminds us that "we are formed of the muck and
slime of that same earth from which we can never be quit."
The images of space man and archaic man express what

Barrett calls man's "ultimate division in our time of need"— our need to sink back to earth at the same time that we leave earth for the emptiness of space. This division is precisely the human condition, a "war of the opposites within us that we cannot escape without becoming less than ourselves."

Barrett insists that the movement into space has no human meaning in itself. It holds out nothing new for man, and even as a technological feat it is probably less important than the development of the internal combustion engine. But space flight has great importance as an imaginative symbol of man's capacity to leave earth behind. All earlier civilizations remained tied to earth—and tied to one degree or another to archaic man and the original well-springs of religion and art. Now we seem headed toward a civilization that can break completely this tie to the primitive past. This is the imaginative leap into the future signified by space exploration, and it is vastly more audacious than the mere physical leap into space. It would surely be man's most daring adventure, his greatest journey. But Barrett suggests that it cannot succeed short of man becoming something different than he is, a figure tied in a deep part of his being to earth and his own primitive past.

In an article called "Re-Entry: Earth Images in Post-Apollo Culture," Daniel C. Noel recalls a cartoon that appeared in the *New York Times* above an excerpt from Barrett's *Time of Need*. In the cartoon an astronaut peers down from the moon upon an earth landscape of four monolithic heads that bring to mind the stone images of Easter Island. The mysterious forms (as well as the equally mysterious rectangular slab that appeared in the film *2001* and the sacred mountain in *Close Encounters of the Third Kind* and René Magritte's surreal painting of a gray rock used on the cover of Norman Mailer's *Of a Fire on the Moon*) cause Noel to wonder why such "sacred stones" frequently appeared in the national imagination at just the time of the Apollo flights to the moon.

The answer, he believes, is that they represent the primitive consciousness that Barrett refers to (or the sunflower forest of Eiseley), a primitive consciousness filled with archetypal reverberations that surfaced now because space exploration had permitted us to look back on ourselves in an entirely new way. The function of the images, Noel writes, is to "teach us at the height of our highest technological leap beyond the bounds of earth that our humanness requires a seemingly outmoded grounding in the dark wet soil of home." In other words, the images paradoxically suggest, at the very moment of departure from earth, the possibility of a new "sensory re-connection to the planet," a new return to an earth of mystery and myth.

This seemed exactly the hope of a variety of scholars who reflected on space exploration: that the journey to the stars would also return us to earth, to a fresh understanding of man's necessary link to the planet. They contemplated a radical altering of the human condition as man left the planet, but characteristically they turned attention to the "miracle" Eiseley hoped for in the rediscovery of the essential grounding of human nature in earth, a rediscovery made possible by the contrast between the sensual satisfactions of earth and the barren universe.

3   Just People

Just before the *Apollo 11* moon landing, Harry Towns, the hero of Bruce Jay Friedman's novel *About Harry Towns* (1974), wonders whether the astronauts went through the same ups and downs as ordinary men:

> Towns wondered if the astronauts went through things like that, whether they had ugly split-ups with wives who subsequently ran off to Dubrovnik, boys who drew pictures of apes leaping from buildings, if they ever wound up scarring men in far-off roadside motels at midnight. His first impulse was to feel no, they didn't. They were too sober and well-rooted for that kind of nonsense.

But the more he considers it, the less certain Towns is that the astronauts were so free of the ordinary human non-sense of his own experience. There were signs, hints, that the astronauts might not be so different:

> But then again, Towns remembered pictures of the pinched and weary faces of some of the astronauts' wives and it became his guess that all wasn't as tidy as it came off in the national magazines. He knew what those long separa-tions for work did to marriages. There was probably no beating the system even if you were a non-ethnic space pioneer and your wife

was an astronautical winner. He decided they
were men, too, some good, some not so hot.
They had experienced failure, ate too much
marinara sauce on occasion, vomited appropriately, lusted after models, worried about being a fag, and about having cancer, even had a
quick ejaculation or two. These thoughts
comforted Harry Towns somewhat as he sat
down on his boy's bed, gave the TV set a few
shots to get it started, and prepared to watch
the fulfillment of man's most ancient dream.

Towns guesses about right. The astronauts' lives, as
they themselves portrayed them, were not so tidy. Their
self-portraits confirm that they were not immune from
contemporary confusions but in fact experienced them
all, from marriage problems and shaky careers and mental
breakdowns through religious anxiety and wayward children and fear of death. Indeed, in their books the astronauts seemed especially eager to establish their link with
the ordinary experience of mankind. They labored to red-
ress the imbalance of media coverage of their exploits in
which they were broadly drawn as heroic figures.* "In the
glory years of space," Walter Cunningham writes in his
book, "what the country kept forgetting was that we were
people." The remark provides a theme line for all the astronaut books. We were just people, the astronauts insist,
who happened to do some spectacular things. "The one
thing we were not," Cunningham adds, "was heroes."

In a popular novel by Maggie Davis called *Eagles* (1980)
an aspiring astronaut nicknamed Moonbird muses raptu-
rously about space flight while watching tapes of *Star
Wars* on his home video unit: "Who saw the beauty and
symmetry in zero, the eternal, constant and challenging

*And in such generally flattering, though informative, accounts of
their own as *We Seven*, published by the Mercury astronauts in 1962,
and *First on the Moon*, published by the *Apollo 11* astronauts in 1970.

void? But *there* was the real fascination and passion. It gave him a fine, calm, almost sweetly desolate feeling to watch the stars spinning around noiselessly out there. Home, earth, was just a watery ball floating above you. Life was the place that began after, not before, the decimal point. He couldn't think of anything more satisfying. Not earthbound, restless, bored ever more. His soul reached out for it." If the real astronauts ever had such soaring thoughts about space flight—let alone actual experience akin to such thoughts—they take pains to suppress them in their books. Instead, they show themselves every bit as earth-bound, as restless, and even as bored as ordinary people.

In another popular novel, Richard Rhodes's *Sons of Earth* (1981), a former Apollo astronaut named "Red" Wainwright has to deal with the abduction of his teen-aged son by a demented drifter. The boy is buried underground in a small box with a limited air supply system, an ironic inversion of the astronaut's capsule flight to the moon, and in the course of Wainwright's hectic efforts to raise the ransom money that eventually frees the boy, Rhodes comments on his career as an astronaut and its aftermath. For Wainwright the moon flight was both a stirring adventure and an experience of rare beauty; but in the swirling publicity of his return to earth, his life fell apart. Ten years later—the setting of the novel—he is a chastened figure, living alone on a small farm, writing about solar energy, and deeply involved with his children. "My children are my treasure," he says. "I value them more than gold, more than fame—more, God knows, than any mark in the record book so temporary and also-ran as walking on the moon." Even the present "pause" in the space program seems to him appropriate. "There's unfinished business down here on the ground, business we ought to attend to before we start floating away into space like pollen. If it's a question of saving the baby or saving the work of art, I'm for saving the baby. Aren't you?"

Rhodes appears to have read the astronauts' books. The accounts they provide of their flying careers and the lives they returned to after their space journeys are not unlike the sober recollections of his fictional hero. Harry Towns would recognize them all, Wainwright and the real astronauts, and find comfort in glimpsing in them his own troublesome self.

Edwin E. "Buzz" Aldrin's subject in *Return to Earth* is the ironic aftermath of his historic *Apollo 11* flight to the moon, what happened when he plunged back to earth. He opens the book with the spacecraft dropping back into the Pacific: "All that precise work was now done and behind us. It would take a couple of years for it to become clear to me, but that day on the USS *Hornet* was actually the start of the trip to the unknown. I had known what to expect on the unknown moon more than I did on the familiar earth." And he ends the book on exactly the same ironic note: "I participated in what will probably be remembered as the greatest technological achievement in the history of this country. I traveled to the moon, but the most significant voyage of my life began when I returned from where no man had been before."

As Aldrin describes it, readjustment to earthly life was a puzzling and nearly disastrous experience. In the book he tries to come to terms with the experience by explaining the difficulties he faced and trying to isolate the causes. The explanation he finally settles on has to do with the attitude toward life he shared with most of the astronauts. Aldrin describes them as "workaholics," men not only with vast capacity for work but with the ability for intense concentration on specific goals. In Aldrin's own case there were many goals, one following the other, leading to the greatest goal of all, the moon landing.

Aldrin was always bent on success. Early in life he learned that "winners won the esteem of their peers and their leaders, losers did not," and so he set out to become a winner. His natural competitiveness was coupled with a no-nonsense personality that found its greatest pleasure in work. "I had the great good fortune," he says, "of entering a business [flying] I truly loved and I was only too happy to talk business at any time, and I had the reputation for doing just that." In his "business" Aldrin's life was a succession of triumphs: West Point honor graduate, Ph.D. from M.I.T., pilot, test pilot, crew member of *Gemini 12*, second man on the moon.

But after all that, what? Aldrin's essential problem, as he comes to recognize it, is that by age forty he has accomplished all there is to accomplish in the flying business—and for a competitive, goal-driven personality that posed a grave difficulty. "What to do next?" he asks. "What possible goal could I add now? There simply wasn't one, and without a goal I was like an inert ping-pong ball being batted about by the whims and motivations of others. I was suffering from what poets have described as the melancholy of all things done." After *Apollo 11*, Aldrin left the space program and tried to pick up his military career as commander of the Air Force Test Pilot School. But it did not work; the goals were no longer there or he could not find them. Nor could he handle the attention of an awed world. His life, quite suddenly, began to unravel. He had an affair with a woman and considered ending his marriage; he worried about "flicker flashes" he had seen on the moon flight and the possibility that they destroyed nerve cells; he feared suicidal tendencies in himself since his grandfather and possibly his mother had been suicides. Finally, he sank into deep depression and underwent psychiatric treatment. He was subsequently passed over for promotion to brigadier general and, as a result, he left the Air Force. He moved to California, became a director of the National Association for Mental Health, and, in part inspired by Senator Thomas Eagleton's acknowledgement of his problems with depression, began his book.

The irony running through Aldrin's account is that his training prepared him for a career that could not last, while his life, for which he had so little training, went on and on. The mystery of living on earth overshadows the mystery of travel to the moon; what to do next with one's life becomes a more perplexing problem than how to walk on the lunar surface. Rather than freeing himself from them, the second man on the moon experiences in abundance all the modern problems. Even the best reason he offers for writing his book is strikingly contemporary: to emerge from the faceless and engineered wonderworld of the astronauts and join the human world of individual personalities and topical concerns. "I wanted," he writes, "to stand up and be counted."

For Aldrin that means, among other things, correcting the unbalanced view of the astronauts presented by the media. The astronauts were hardly the "simon-pure guys" the nation was led to believe. Aldrin says that they attracted "groupies" like rock musicians; some resisted the temptation, but many resisted and then gave in, himself included. And their domestic lives were far removed from the tidy images sent out to the public. There were long and difficult family separations during the training period, problems with children, and terror for the wives during the space flights. At the mandatory press conference on the lawn of his home after the landing of *Apollo 11*, Aldrin recalls that his wife told reporters she felt "thrilled, proud, and happy." Later she told him she had lied; she was really "scared to death and enormously relieved." Around the house the heroic astronaut, Aldrin says about himself, was more often than not "inattentive, tired, and asleep on the den sofa by nine o'clock."

About his experience on the moon Aldrin offers little that is memorable. He felt "buoyant and was full of goose pimples" when he stepped down on the moon's surface. His first act was to kick the lunar dust, intrigued by its peculiar property of flying out in exactly even distances.

His second was to urinate in the spacesuit apparatus. Neil Armstrong, he says with a rare touch of lightheartedness, "might have been the first man to step on the moon, but I was the first to pee in his pants on the moon." Before this unremarkable moment, while waiting in the landing craft with Armstrong while Michael Collins circled the moon in the spacecraft, Aldrin recounts the single most unusual incident in his book—his reception of communion on the moon.

He had brought with him a small amount of wine, a wafer, and a chalice, and with them took communion while reading from a card on which he had written a passage from the Book of John. The act is all the more striking since nothing in the book quite prepares the reader for it, nor does Aldrin offer an adequate explanation. He mentions his membership in the Presbyterian Church and his friendship with a Houston minister, but he gives no special emphasis to his religious background or convictions. Mailer in *Of a Fire on the Moon* writes obscurely of Aldrin as both a "high priest" and a "technologue," and he interprets his reception of communion as a ritual ceremony meant to embrace the machine with traditionalist faith. But it seems more likely that the communion service is simply tied to Aldrin's willingness, unusual among the astronauts, to think of the symbolic aspects of the moon flight and celebrate them in ritual ways.

In a telecast from *Apollo 11* after the moon landing, Aldrin, Armstrong, and Collins each gave a brief talk. Collins stressed the intricacy of the spacecraft equipment while Armstrong thanked everyone involved in the mission. Aldrin began by saying he wanted to discuss a "few of the more symbolic aspects" of the flight, and observed that the flight "stands as a symbol of the insatiable curiosity of all mankind to explore the unknown." In a speech before Congress after the flight, Aldrin returned to a symbolic conception of *Apollo 11*. "Our steps in space," he said, "have been a symbol of this country's way of life as we open our doors and windows to the world to view our successes and failures and as we share with all nations our discovery."

Finally, it is neither ritual celebrations nor symbolic interpretations of the moon landing that occupy the center of Aldrin's account, but the practical problem of human adjustment that attends his return to earth. And the heart of the problem is that the success of *Apollo 11* cannot be duplicated; the end of the flight meant the end of a career, the only career Aldrin ever wanted. On the flight back to Houston after the landing in the Pacific, Aldrin says the "enormity of it all" began to sink into him: "I had often thought of it before, and Neil and I had talked about it off and on during training. But there was something different about it now: the trip was over, the goal accomplished, and so much time and effort had been put into it. Before, thoughts had been focused on the technical achievement ahead of us. All that precise work was now done and behind us." For Aldrin, as he portrays himself in his book, it seems unlikely that anything in the future can approximate the pleasure of the precise work needed to reach the moon, nor any activity seem half so worthwhile as walking on the moon. Two years after the appearance of his book, Aldrin told a *National Observer* reporter that sometimes he "gazes up at the moon and mutters to himself: 'You son of a bitch . . . you're the one that got me in all this trouble.' " The irony of Aldrin's story is that the moment of his great achievement, the second man to walk on the moon, was also the moment that precipitated the decline of his career and personal life. Going to the moon had the effect of returning him to earth, a shattering experience that brought him close to total ruin.

To lean that James Irwin took communion on the moon would not be surprising, and in fact Irwin says he felt a strong desire for a religious service during the flight of *Apollo 15. To Rule the Night* (1973) is an account of spiritual awakening; it tells of a man's discovery of his spiritual mission in life through the experience of a moon mission. Throughout his book Irwin distinguishes between the "technical flight" and the "spiritual flight," and it is always the latter, the movement toward God and the acceptance of God's plan for one's life, that matters most. God rules the night, Irwin discovers; his power reigns absolute in the universe. The corollary is that God establishes each man's destiny and that a man's true task, his real career, is to discover what that destiny is and embrace it with love and trust.

Although Irwin's book differs from Aldrin's in its direct religious concern, there is a basic similarity between the two. Both concentrate more on what happened after the moon venture, on the return to earth, than on the space experience itself. "The Lord," Irwin writes, "wanted me to go to the moon so I could come back and do something more important with my life than fly airplanes." And like Aldrin, Irwin laments that nothing about his training as a flyer or astronaut prepared him for the aftermath of the moon. "The only thing I wasn't prepared for," he observes, "was the spiritual impact of the voyage to the moon."

On the moon Irwin distinctly felt God's presence. He says that the sight of the small, distant earth "looking so fragile, so delicate, that if you touched it with a finger it would crumble and fall apart" has to change a man, "has to make a man appreciate the creation of God and the love of God." But there is too much work in space for reflection, and impressions are simply stored in the memory, overwhelmed by activity. Even with his return to earth, Irwin confined his remarks in news conferences and speeches to the technical aspects of the flight. But he continued to ponder his experience of God on the moon, "trying to put together the message I wanted to share with the world." For the first time in his life he began examining his past, trying to "find out who I was and what was happening to me."

Two thing stand out in Irwin's reconstruction of things past: a seemingly shallow attitude toward life and marital troubles. Irwin had a fascination with flashy, and preferably red, cars during his pre-Apollo years; about his red Corvette he exclaims, "man, that's living." The remark suggests Irwin's school-boy fascination with machines and a general naiveté that eventually would get him in trouble with NASA and provide the space program with its only public scandal. The *Apollo 15* crew—David Scott, Alfred Worden, and Irwin—took aboard the spacecraft some 400 unauthorized envelopes. During the third day on the moon the stamps were cancelled and the date imprinted, August 2, 1971; after splashdown the envelopes were signed by the astronauts. The three astronauts keep 100 envelopes each and another 100 were sent to a West German businessman. The idea was that the envelopes would be sold as collectors' items after the Apollo program was over and the money, some $8,000 for each of the astronauts, used to set up trust funds for the education of their children. But when the envelopes went on the market soon after the flight, the story got out. After a Congressional investigation, the crew was officially reprimanded by NASA.

The envelope episode (called by Michael Collins the "shady stamps-for-sale deal") seems an incredibly naive blunder on the part of the astronauts. But Irwin passes lightly over it in his book, reflecting neither on the ethics involved nor on why the astronauts got into the scheme in the first place. Neither does he indicate any regret. He says that Scott, who had enjoyed a high reputation in the astronaut corps, "must have suffered every sort of agony throughout the envelope episode," but he does not indicate that he himself experienced any suffering at all.

About his two marriages Irwin is more revealing. While in flight training he fell in love with a young girl who was a Roman Catholic—a considerable problem for someone with Irwin's admitted anti-Catholic feelings. He refused to marry the girl until she gave up her religion; when she consulted a priest following a quarrel, he abruptly broke off the marriage. "It really torqued me off," he says. "I couldn't accept that." The considerable irony in the story, as Irwin sees, is that at this stage of his life he had no strong religious convictions of his own. After the divorce Irwin fell in love again, this time with a Seventh-Day Adventist. He admits that he was as "anti-Adventist as I was anti-Catholic," and the new marriage was threatened by religious differences. Irwin and his wife tried Presbyterian and Methodist churches as a common religious meeting ground, but his wife could not give up the Adventist church nor could he abandon his aversion to it.

During the months of his astronaut training his "anger and hostility about the home situation" kept him constantly unsettled. He and his wife considered divorce, and many times he thought about leaving the Apollo program because he felt the emotional turmoil of his domestic life hindered his concentration. Seven months before the moon flight Irwin's wife finally decided to file for divorce, but according to her own account "the Lord turned her around, and that He pushed her and kicked her all over the place," and so she determined to stick it out. From this close point the marriage began to improve, and following the space flight Irwin's wife played a major role in the direction his life took after he accepted his experience of God on the moon.

Irwin began going out on weekends to speak at churches, even addressing a rally of 50,000 Southern Baptists in the Houston Astrodome. From telling about his spiritual experiences on the moon he soon moved to inviting "the audiences to come forward and make a decision

for Jesus Christ." The stipends for his speaking engage-
ments went to the Jim Irwin Missionary Fund. Finally, as
pressure mounted in NASA about the unauthorized envelopes, Irwin left the Air Force and took up a career as an
evangelist. His wife explained the move to him as the
work of divine providence. "It was just like the hand of
God, giving you a push," she told him. "He is saying,
'That's all, Charley. Get out and do *My* thing for *Me!*' "
With the help of a minister friend and the Southern Bap-
tist Church, Irwin established a non-profit enterprise
called High Flight.* He and his wife took to the road full
time, speaking around the world. In his message Irwin says
he tried to visualize the earth as about the size of a basket-
ball and them locate himself exactly where he was with the
audience at that moment. "One time," he writes, "when I
was praying this way, I could see a great hand in space,
and it was directing a light onto the earth right at the spot
where I was at that time. So now when I ask people to
accept Jesus Christ, I ask for God's Spirit to give these
people a new light in their lives."

In 1973 Irwin had a serious heart attack. His wife interpreted it for him as "God taking charge again," and Irwin
concludes: "Somehow my Mission Director was changing
my flight plan. I know that He has a plan for my life. It's
my business just to wait on Him, and He will give me my
orders." In the book's epilogue he adds that the heart attack has made him more dependent on God and better able
to accept his own weaknesses. It also has improved his
domestic life. But the future of High Flight is left in
doubt. Irwin says it will depend on others taking up the
speaking work he is no longer able to bear alone. For him-

---

*The name comes from the title of a poem by John Magee popular
among flyers; Collins took a typed copy of it with him on *Apollo 11.*
The poem concludes: "And, while with silent, lifting mind I've trod/
The high untrespassed sanctity of space,/ Put out my hand, and
touched the face of God."

self, he professes resignation. "I know I need help," he ends the book, "and I am willing to accept it. I am grateful as the Lord reveals His plan for this flight, the Highest Flight of all."*

Michael Collins's *Carrying the Fire* (1974) is the best of the astronaut books, but in some ways it is also the least interesting given the reader's desire for drama equal to the high theater of the moon flights. The book offers no revelations: Collins does not experience God in the vicinity of the moon nor an ironic return to earth; he does not have a nervous breakdown nor separate from his wife nor have a heart attack. Nor does he take himself very seriously. He even manages flashes of humor.

The straightforward, unassuming approach Collins takes in telling his story may have something to do with his position in *Apollo 11*—not a moon walker but the lone orbiter, manning the space vehicle while Armstrong and Aldrin performed their historic feats, clearly the third man of the famous three. Irwin speculates that the lives of lunar-module pilots like him and Aldrin were more changed by the moon flights than those of commanders like Armstrong or command-module pilots like Collins because the limited duties of lunar-module pilots gave them "more time to look out the windows, to register what they saw and felt, and to absorb it." At any event, Collins has no spectacular experience to relate, either on the moon or back on earth, and consequently he offers a more detailed account then either Aldrin or Irwin of what actually happened on a space flight.

In a letter to Collins after *Apollo 11*, Charles Lindbergh suggested that Collins's experience in space must have been more meaningful than that of Aldrin or Armstrong

---

*In 1983 Irwin was climbing Mt. Ararat in Turkey in search of some evidence of the biblical Noah's ark.

because of his total solitude while they walked on the moon. Lindbergh wrote:

> But it seems to me you had an experience of in some ways greater profundity—the hours you spent orbiting the moon alone, and with more time for contemplation. What a fantastic experience it must have been—alone looking down on another celestial body, like a god of space! There is a quality of aloneness that those who have not experienced it cannot know—to be alone and then to return to one's fellow men once more. You have experienced an aloneness unknown to man before. I believe you will find that it lets you think and sense with greater clarity. Sometime in the future, I would like to listen to your conclusions in this respect.

Collins reports the Lindbergh letter but resolutely refuses to be drawn into such a grand conception of his experience. He has far too much humorous detachment to permit himself any special conception of his experience in space, let alone the role of a "god of space." He accepts the observation attributed to NASA administrator Dr. Thomas Paine that the Apollo program was a "triumph of the squares" and refuses to sum up his moon experience with expressions, as he remarks, of "poetry or magic." He does, however, tell of efforts to capture his feelings about space in poetry, and provides an example:

> Cold stones jumbled in a heap.
> Lifeless plains, sharing only the sun,
> With a verdant recollection I must keep,
> Till I next see one:
> One penny, one peony, one misty waterfall.
> For me a choice—to hear a voice,
> Or slip by it all.

Near the end of the book Collins also admits that his experience has to some extent set him apart from other men. He has seen the "ultimate black of infinity in a stillness undisturbed by any living thing" and so possesses "this secret, this precious thing, that I will always carry with me." But he will not let himself dwell on such thoughts. "I didn't find God on the moon," he writes with apparent reference to the accounts of Aldrin and Irwin, "nor has my life changed dramatically in any other basic way." Thus he keeps the focus throughout the book, as he announces in the preface, on "an insider's factual and simple explanation of how the machines operated, who operated them, and what it was like living in an artificial, high-pressure environment." For Collins the flight to the moon was fundamentally a complex and sometimes scary technological achievement.

The nature of the book was foreshadowed by Collins's comments during the final television session aboard *Apollo 11* when he called attention to the difficulties of the flight. "This trip of ours to the moon may have looked, to you, simple or easy," he began. "I'd like to assure you *that* has not been the case." Repeatedly in the book he returns to the complexity of the equipment and the many possibilities for human and mechanical error. Of his earlier *Gemini 10* flight he recalls that "hardly an hour would pass without a fresh opportunity for disaster."

The difficulties, Collins admits, spawned fear—but fear not so much of physical harm as professional failure, fear of embarrassing oneself in the eyes of colleagues. The astronauts' lengthy training in simulators was designed to prepare them for all eventualities, but for Collins a lingering fear always was present that a situation would arise that he would not be prepared for or that a complicated maneuver would not be expertly made. This was something the astronauts could not fully communicate to the public. Only those inside the program, Collins says, "knew the opportunities we had to fail," and he adds that he acutely "felt this pressure, this awesome sense of responsibility weighing me down, this completely negative sensation, this commandment which said, 'Thou shalt not screw up.' "

Only once does Collins admit to plain visceral terror—when the landing vehicle carrying Aldrin and Armstrong is about to leave the moon for rendezvous with the orbiting spacecraft. If the maneuver is not successful Collins must return to earth alone. He writes about the moment: "If they fail to rise from the surface, or crash back into it, I am not going to commit suicide; I am coming home, forthwith, but I will be a marked man for life and I know it. Almost better not to have the option I enjoy." When it finally appears that the rendezvous will be successful, Collins's relief is immense. Even to him the feat seems incredible: "Jesus, we really *are* going to carry this thing off! For the first time since I was assigned to this incredible flight six months ago, for the first time I feel that it *is* going to happen."

Collins makes clear that, due to the hazards involved, the astronauts were preoccupied during space flights with the desire that everything go precisely as planned. They did not want a confrontation with the unexpected. Nothing comforts them more than the discovery that space or the moon is just as they were trained to expect during the simulations on earth. About the moon-landing day Collins remarks: "If we were bullfighters, we would call it the moment of truth, but all I want is a moment of no surprises." And that is what *Apollo 11* was, a flight without surprises—and so a wholly successful flight. Aldrin sums up the flight in terms identical to Collins's: "The voyage to the moon was conducted within nearly half a second of the flight plan. Of all the various midcourse corrections it was possible to make en route to and from the moon, we had used only two. The training and preparation was such that even the unfamilar surface of the moon was very nearly as we had been led to expect. I realized I wasn't in the simulator and it was a good bit more real, but virtually nothing was unexpected."

Collins's emphasis on the moon flight itself rather than the earthly aftermath allows him to pay some attention to the relationships among the astronauts. When Aldrin and Armstrong return to the spacecraft after their moon walks, Collins is so relieved he almost kisses them; but, embarrassed, he catches himself and simply shakes their hands. The scene suggests Collins's general view that the astronauts were "amiable strangers" to one another. He portrays the exchanges among them as friendly but marked by business-like detachment, even after the heated competition for crew selection was over. Although Collins considers himself a loner, he would have preferred a closer relationship with Aldrin and Armstrong. He felt a "bit freakish" about the tendency of the *Apollo 11* crew to transmit only essential information rather than thoughts and feelings. Nonetheless, he apparently did little himself to bridge the gaps of feeling among the crew and finally summarizes his feelings about Aldrin and Armstrong in distant, guarded terms.

Despite Collins's insistence that he was not deeply changed by his experience in space, he ends his book with a moving recollection of the moon and a recognition that it changed his perception of earth. He says there are two moons for him now, the small bright disc he sees from his backyard and the huge moon he remembers, a three-dimensional moon that bulges forward in the middle and is scarred, desolate, and monotonous. He recalls as well how small and fragile earth looked from the moon, and this suggests to him, as it has to other astronauts, a fresh concern with the planet's environment and an impatience with political and economic divisions.

In *The Adventurer* (1974), a study of the role of heroic adventure in the Western world, Paul Zweig writes of the astronauts: "They are perfect—all too perfect?—images of the brave, loyal, individualistic, law-abiding, personally powerful man America wants to admire. If someone made a robot portrait of the perfect citizen, it would resemble an astronaut. The astronaut is a vanishing point for our flawed selves; he is a hero. We tell our sons to be like him." Walter Cunningham's *The All-American Boys* (1977) is devoted to debunking just such a view of the astronauts as ideal types. A crew member of *Apollo 7*, Cunningham explains in a preface that the heroic image of the astronauts was flattering and some of them encouraged it; but it was an unliveable image, one in which the astronauts felt themselves trapped. His book is designed to set the astronauts free by revealing that, as he puts it, "some of history's greatest deeds were accomplished, and a remarkable adventure was fulfilled, by men who were all too human in their weaknesses as well as their strengths."

Like Tom Wolfe in *The Right Stuff* (a work published two years after Cunningham's book and perhaps considerably influenced by it), Cunningham points to the central importance of flying in understanding the astronauts. He says that most of them came into the space program simply because they were flyers and it was "the best game going" at the time. The nature of the flying game is at the core of most of the traits Cunningham singles out in himself and other astronauts: intense competitiveness; ruthless ambition; naiveté about business matters; sexual adventurousness; low-key emotional responses.

Most of the astronauts were already shaped by their competitive success in military flying; as a result, competition was a "universal thread" running through the astronaut corps. Even a request for a urine sample became a test of who could fill the biggest bottle. The rivalry frequently carried over into efforts to undermine the standing of others in the astronaut hierarchy, all in the hope of improving chances for an attractive space ride. Cunningham gives a list of "astropolitics" commandments that boil down to a single command: "Do unto others as they would do unto you, but do it first." Back-stabbing is

made to seem a normal feature of the competitive flying
game, but it became all the more intense due to the mystery surrounding the selection of space crews. "We never
were able to spell out the process by which one made it to a
prime crew assignment," Cunningham says, "but we concluded that there was no science to it." Consequently, the
astronauts tried not only to measure up in performance
but to gain any advantage they could on their rivals, and
by any means available. If the astronauts didn't invent
"gamesmanship," Cunningham observes, "we sure per-
fected it as an art form."

The astronauts found themselves in another kind of
competition as well, one for which they were less prepared. They were the objects of heated social attention
from the wealthy and powerful, and in most such situa-
tions their modest military pay put them in a position of
acute financial inequality. The economic gap between the
astronauts and their admirers was intensified by the
NASA setting in Houston, a city marked by splashy displays of wealth. One way the astronauts managed to live
beyond their means was by accepting all manner of gifts
and favors. An insurance company gave them four per
cent mortgages, allowing them to buy homes they other-
wise could not afford. And there were publishing con-
tracts with Time-Life and Field Enterprises that in some
instances brought in more than their government salaries.
But the astronauts also were tempted into business deals
for which they were not prepared. In some cases they were
exploited by companies for their name value; in others
they went into flimsy schemes because it never occurred to
them that their rich friends could make serious business
mistakes. Looking back, Cunningham says, most of the
business deals ended badly and most of the astronauts
were "singed" in the process.

What Cunningham calls the "sexual fallout" of the
space program was another side of the heady new world in
which the astronauts found themselves. As military pilots
used to long absences from home, sexual adventuring was

nothing new to them; but with their celebrity status the temptations multiplied, and Cunningham agrees with Aldrin that few of the astronauts resisted. Most of them understood their sexual opportunities as additional per-quisites of their situation and decided, as Cunningham puts it, to cash in. For others, sexual adventuring was an expression of the restlessness of flyers with the routine technical demands of astronaut training. In any case, the astronauts emerge from Cunningham's account as a good deal less than the dedicated family men of popular imagination.

As a group, the pilots who entered the space program were tight-lipped fellows who habitually understated their feelings. Predictably, they had little to say about the emotional aspects of their space rides. Cunningham sug-gests that their emotional restraint also had something to do with not wanting to give others a possible competitive advantage; it was an attempt to live up to what they be-lieved NASA required of them. But in reality, Cun-ningham says, the astronauts shared a "spiritual com-mitment to adventure"; they had strong feelings about space flight that were akin to religious feelings. In retro-spect, he believes the astronauts missed an opportunity in not expressing their exhiliration over "exploring what-ever was out there," and he points to the thrill of adven-ture as one of the important benefits of the space program. But his own account deals sparingly with emotions in space. His emphasis, rather, is on the gap between the heroic image of the astronauts and the quite ordinary reality.

The strongest emotion the astronauts seem to have ex-perienced in space is fear of performing badly. In the fly-ing business, Cunningham says, echoing Collins, death is a secondary consideration to the fear of "making an ass of yourself—especially in front of your peers." But it was a fear that had to be concealed. The astronauts were at the top of their profession and the competition was intense; the slightest mistake could be a major setback, blocking what Cunningham calls "that one more flight every pilot craves." So attention was firmly fixed not on the mythic dimensions of the flights or the extraordinary sights of outer space but on carrying out complex assignments under the close scrutiny of peers, all the while holding one's breath that one would not be found wanting.

If in popular imagination the astronauts were All-American boys, their stoical wives were All-Americans too—brave, supportive, as devoted as their husbands to NASA and the mission in space. But that is not the way it comes out in Betty Grissom's *Starfall* (1974), an autobiographical portrait (though told mostly in the third person with a co-author's help) of an astronaut wife who endured long separations from her husband, raised her sons virtually alone, suffered through one of the space program's tragic failures, and finally felt herself abandoned by NASA and the other astronauts.

On January 27, 1967, astronauts Gus Grissom, Ed White, and Roger Chaffee were killed in a flash fire in an Apollo spacecraft during testing at the Kennedy Space Center in Florida. The accident abruptly ended Grissoms's successful career as one of the seven original Mercury astronauts, the second American in space aboard *Liberty Bell 7*, and along with John Young a crew member on the first Gemini flight (the latter story related by Grissom in a book for young people, *Gemini!*, published in 1968). With her husband's death Betty Grissom's devotion to the closed world of military flying and later the astronauts corps, described in the book by the term "togethersville," slowly began to unravel. But at first his death seemed only another of the absences that had marked their marriage during the astronaut years. "Well, I'm going to miss the phone calls," she thought. "That's mostly what I had of him. The phone calls."

With two sons to raise and an income of less than $5,000 a year, her living situation was difficult. When there was a squabble among the astronauts about how much money should go to the widows from a documentary film on the astronauts and their families, she thought she was being "dumped by the wayside" and as a result felt hurt and angry, realizing that the "astronauts didn't give a damn about the widows." Finally, she went to an attorney in Houston to bring suit for damages in her husband's death, breaking the peer-enforced "code of togethersville" that decreed "you should accept your loss in silence, bear up, speak no evil, don't rock the boat, be noble and sacrifice your life to the good of government and military."

When the suit was filed (just short of four years after Grissom's death) for $10 million in damages from North American Rockwell, the maker of the spacecraft, it drew national attention and created a heated controversy. The widows of White and Chaffee refused to join Betty Grissom in the suit and, under the erroneous assumption that it was the government being sued, her patriotism was sharply attacked. But she kept on with the suit and finally after much legal maneuvering an out-of-court settlement was reached that brought her $350,000. The two other widows later settled for the same amount.

In a final chapter of the book Betty Grissom displays her patriotism and her continuing, though muted, interest in the space program. When she tries to sum up her feelings she simply says, "I hate it that Gus is gone, but I guess the program was worth it." But the hurt and anger, the loss of a sense of "togethersville," is still apparent. She mentions a moon rock on display at the Johnson Space Center in Houston and it causes her to wonder how many of the astronauts have moon rocks in their possession—and then to remark: "I think the widows and children should have some presented to them. After all, our husbands gave their lives."

A chapter of Cunningham's book is devoted to the problem of "hyphenated astronauts": the scientists who eventually entered the astronaut corps and competed with the fighter pilots who dominated the space program. Cunningham calls the tug of war between the pilots and scientists— or between the goals of technology and those of science—the "real clash" within the space program. At first, the pilots were clearly victors in the struggle; thirty-two fighter pilots went into space before the first scientist (Harrison Schmitt on the final Apollo mission). But with the end of the Apollo program and the beginning of Skylab, it was apparent that a transition was underway that stressed not only flying skill in astronauts but the ability to carry on scientific investigations in space. Nonetheless, the scientist-astronaut still had to contend with the dominant emphasis on flying skills within the Astronaut Office at NASA, with the result that of the first seventeen scientist-astronauts brought into the program, three quit within the first year and two more were dropped.

One of those who quit was Brian O'Leary, a planetary astronomer. His book, *The Making of an Ex-Astronaut* (1970), describes in step-by-step detail the process whereby he applied for the second group of scientist-astronauts (and the sixth group of astronauts) while finishing graduate study, was selected and went through ground training in Houston, and eventually gave up one month into the mandatory flight training. Flying was the main sticking point. O'Leary and others were not only required to learn to fly but, he believed, "to *love* jet piloting," and this turned out to be more than he could manage. He was constantly air sick and had trouble with the mechanics of flying; the one-in-five chance of killing himself in a high-performance jet was never far from his mind. Moreover, he could not accept the connection between jet flying and his role as a scientist in space. He thought ground simulation and occasional jet rides were sufficient flying experience, and that the time saved in pilot training could best be used in preparing for the science he would do in space. When he finally called Deke Slayton in Houston to resign from the program, he told him: "I guess flying just isn't my cup of tea."

There were other problems as well. Physically, Houston compared badly with his adopted city of San Francisco ("heat, humidity, smog, gray skies, rain, flat terrain, gumbo, dish keys, and general dullness"), and he felt that the concentration of the NASA program in Houston removed him too much from the mainstream of scientific activity. There also was his "rebellious spirit" that kept him at odds with the military regimentation that dominated NASA. But what O'Leary emphasizes in his book is the division between scientists and pilots in the space program. He acknowledges the importance of pilot skill in the moon flights, but he also points to scientific errors in the descriptions of the moon given by pilot-astronauts and mistakes in their scientific samplings. In their space photographs, he finds the astronauts "shutter-happy tourists" with a "fixation on the miniscule earth" as a result of their finding the lunar landscape barren and uninviting.

What O'Leary finally calls for is less bias in NASA in favor of pilot skills and greater attention to the importance of science in space—for an equal role in space flights for those scientists like himself who do not thrill to guiding a supersonic T-38 through high skies. He suggests that NASA, dominated by the Office of Manned Space Flight, has concentrated on the question of what man can do in space. For O'Leary the better question is how best a mission can be performed, whether manned or unmanned, and what it adds to an understanding of the universe.

In a foreword to Collins's book, Charles Lindbergh refers to the effect on human awareness of great technological developments. He seems to have in mind near-mystical breakthroughs in perception, radically new advances in consciousness. But the accounts of the astronauts testify to something quite different—not to psychological or spiritual leaps forward but to personal returns to a time-worn sense of human limitation.

William Pogue, a member of the crew of *Skylab 3*, was reported in the press as saying that his experience in space made him acutely aware of his human limits. He learned during his 84-day flight that he could not work in the mechanically efficient way he had on earth; he discovered he was going to make mistakes and that it was necessary to accept such weakness in himself. Oddly, at the very peak of his professional career as a flyer, Pogue gained a sense of his shortcomings that was not apparent to him before. In their books the astronauts reach similar conclusions; space flight teaches them not only that the earth is vulnerable but they are too. Only O'Leary, an astronaut who did not fly in space, seems untouched by this fresh sense of human limitation.

Part of the awareness comes simply from the knowledge that they have been to the top of the flying profession and never again will have jobs equal to it. The astronauts who fly in space seem to experience the melancholy sensation of all things done; they confront the problem of preventing the rest of their lives from becoming anticlimactic. But the space flights themselves, and not simply the experience of returning to earth, appear to contribute to the astronauts' sense of personal limitation. In space the astronauts function as a team, a team that extends far beyond the crew members in the capsule; they recognize their dependence on an army of technicians and sophisticated machinery that is beyond their complete manipulation or comprehension. The full weight of this dependence seems to come only when the long training is over and the crew is finally alone in space. Only in narrowly confined ways can they control their own destinies once the spacecraft is launched. Alan Bean, the fourth man to walk on the moon, likened the sense of vulnerability experienced by the astronauts in space to the feeling of being "out on a limb where your natural instincts can't help." He told the *National Observer*: "There's just the three of you in this little metal can, and you look out the window and see the earth far away, and you realize that you can't intuitively get back home. For the first time in your life, perhaps, you're out on a limb where your natural instincts can't help. If something goes wrong, the alternatives go down to maybe two: Either the ground is going to tell you how to get it home, or somehow you're going to figure it out with your computer."

Nothing at last could be more inappropriate in the eyes of the astronauts who have had this humbling experience than a conception of themselves as gods of space. Even the role of earthly heroes in the Lindbergh mold leaves them distinctly uncomfortable. In their books they want, with Aldrin, to stand up and be counted as ordinary people with ordinary lives and ordinary problems. Perhaps nothing better establishes their absorption in the life of the time more than their insistence on their flawed humanity; it is their disclosure of weakness, they believe, not the concealing of it nor the transcendence of it, that reveals them as authentically contemporary men.* Harry Towns does indeed have it about right. As they portray themselves, the men who fulfilled "man's most ancient dream" turn out to be "men, too, some good, some not so hot."

---

*Even a Russian cosmonaut, who spent a record 211 days in space aboard the research station *Salyut 7*, was willing to reveal a less than heroic side. Excerpts from the diary of Valentin Lebedev, published in the Communist Party newspaper *Pravda*, indicate that he slept badly in space, longed for his home and family, and struggled to control his anger with his fellow cosmonaut. He found that he could ease the strain of the seven-month journey only by observing the beauties of earth through the windows of the space station.

4   A Meaning to Us

Just before the *Apollo 11* moon landing, an *Esquire* article speculated on proper words for the first astronaut to say as he stepped onto the moon. The assumption of the article was that nothing much of importance would be said; to the author, William E. Honan, it already was "perfectly clear—it would be folly to deny it longer—that while the space program is poised on the brink of a truly epoch-making triumph of engineering, it is also headed for a rhetorical wreck." The immediate source of the wreckage was the lack of imagination and perception on the part of astronauts who had failed to tell us what space was really like. All we had gotten from them was that it was "beautiful." They had used the word, the writer observed, "like a Boy Scout jackknife, for every imaginable task."

Prominent literary figures were quoted on what they wished to hear from the first man on the moon. A few offered serious remarks but most, in the spirit of the article, did not. Kurt Vonnegut was characteristically whimsical: "Was this the face that launch'd a thousand ships?" Truman Capote was uncharacteristically brief: "So far so good." Joseph Heller was simply bored: "I'd like to hear nothing; the chances are I won't be listening. I'm more interested in what Joe Namath or George Sauer has to say about anything, and I hope the moon landing doesn't take place during a Jet football game and interrupt the telecast."

Probably few American writers of the time were as disinterested in *Apollo 11* as Heller claimed to be. Nonetheless, the implication of the *Esquire* article—that as a rhetorical failure space exploration offered little inspiration to the literary imagination—seemed plausible enough. All that writers knew about the new ocean of space came second hand—and second hand from spokesmen hardly notable for their way with words. In *Of a Fire on the Moon*, Mailer laments that it would not be until men who "spoke like Shakespeare" rode the rockets that we would possess an appropriate response to the adventure in space—and that was surely "many eons" away. For the present the only guides were astronauts who, while expert and courageous, were "philosophically naive, jargon-ridden, and resolutely divorced from any language with grandeur to match the proportions of [their] endeavor."

Yet even had the astronauts provided richly Shakespearean accounts of their adventures, literary minds still might have found space exploration a less than compelling subject. The accounts surely would emphasize the achievements of engineering rather than, as Saul Bellow's Artur Sammler would say, the adventures of the spirit. Bellow has instructed us that the real business of art is with the individual's sense of the peculiar significance of his own existence, a business increasingly hard to transact in a technological world that often seems bent on reducing the individual to a collective identity. Indeed, the astronauts themselves were hard to recognize as individual figures. Behind them were armies of skilled technicians and backup crews who rehearsed missions in the same manner as prime crews. "Up there in orbit," Wright Morris remarked about the astronauts, "they're as alone as all get out—but alone was not how they got there. The big thing they did was agree to the trip. All the king's horses and all the king's men then went ahead and did it."

So whatever the nature of the astronauts' reports on outer space, the literary imagination, tuned to the personal mysteries of inner space, seemed unlikely to find

much of interest in space exploration. More intriguing
the heroics of a football team on a rectangle of earth than
Aldrin and Armstrong on the moon. If the latter provided
subject matter at all, it would be for bravura journalists
like Mailer and Tom Wolfe; let them wrestle with feats of
engineering and the programmed psyches of the astronauts. But in fact novelists and poets did not shrink entirely from a literary concern with space exploration. A number of imaginative writers drew it into their work, making
it their direct subject or, more frequently, employing it as
background for their primary concerns.

In Wright Morris's novel *The Fork River Space Project*
(1977), a character says: "The view into space is unending,
and a measure of man's creative cunning, but the view
from space compels the awe that will enlarge man's finite
nature." The remark suggests in a particularly felicitous
way the common use of space exploration in literary
works as a means of turning attention back to earth and
earthly life. Rather than the view into space, it is the view
from space leading back to earth and its ordinary concerns
that has occupied literary minds, a view sometimes inspiring awe in that the earth is seen as all the more mysterious
and precious, sometimes simply emphasizing earth as the
only meaningful setting for the human drama. Appropriately, in Archibald MacLeish's poem "Voyage to the
Moon," it is not the arrived-upon moon that instills
wonder but the sight of earth from the moon:

> Now, the fourth day evening, we descend,
> make fast, set foot at last upon her beaches,
> stand in her silence, lift our heads and see
> above her, wanderer in her sky,
> a wonder to us past the reach of wonder,
> a light beyond our lights, our lives, the rising
> earth,
>
> a meaning to us,
>
> O, a meaning!

But within such a broad return-to-earth conception of our space journeys—the tendency to view them, in light of "the rising earth," as some form of "a meaning to us"—there remained significant variation in the particular ways writers drew upon the events and effects of the age of space.

In John Updike's *Rabbit Redux* (1971), space exploration is used to create a topical texture for the novel and, more importantly, to serve as ironic counterpoint to the main action of the work. References to space exploration and especially the *Apollo 11* moon landing appear throughout the text. For example, Harry "Rabbit" Angstrom and his son Nelson have an exchange in the jargon of astronauts:

> "Want to head home?"
>
> "Negative, Pop." He drowsily grins at his own wit.
>
> Rabbit extends the joke. "The time is twenty-one hours. We better rendezvous with our spacecraft."
>
> But the spacecraft is empty: a long empty box in the blackness of Penn Villas, slowly spinning in the void, its border beds half-weeded. The kid is frightened to go home. So is Rabbit.

Likewise, Rabbit's father, watching television in a bar after work, is momentarily characterized against a background of the moon mission: "Pop stands whittled by the great American glare, squinting in the manna of blessings that come down from the government, shuffling from side to side in nervous happiness that his day's work is done, that a beer is inside him, that Armstrong is above him, that the U.S. is the crown and stupefication of human history. Like a piece of grit in the lauching pad, he has done his part."

But the more significant use of space in the novel is to establish an ironic contrast between the epic adventure of Armstrong and his colleagues and the ordinary lives of the novel's earthbound characters. As workingmen in the bar watch television repeats of the blast-off of *Apollo 11*, Updike notes that although "dark along the bar they murmur" at the spectacle, they themselves "have not been lifted, they are left here." Throughout the novel space flight, whatever its historic importance, is shown to have little relation to flattened, troubled lives; Updike's characters struggle on unlifted, unburdened, and it is their lives that command the reader's attention and sympathy.

Later in the novel's opening section (entitled "Pop/Mom/Moon") Rabbit Angstrom watches the evening news and it is all about space, "all about emptiness." A panel of experts discuss the significance of the approaching moon landing, offering analogies with Columbus, "but as far as Rabbit can see it's the exact opposite: Columbus flew blind and hit something, these guys see exactly what they're aiming at and it's a big round nothing." For Rabbit the flight to the moon is of little consequence since it has no bearing on his dimly understood struggle to keep some slight foothold on the land Columbus hit.

At the end of the section the triumphant moon landing is set in direct contrast to the accelerating failure of Rabbit's life. Rabbit and his son are at his parents' home for a birthday party for his ailing mother. In her bedroom they watch television as the moon landing takes place, Updike quoting at length conversations of the astronauts coming from Tranquillity Base. But Rabbit's thoughts, untranquil, keep drifting off to his wife who has just deserted him for a Toyota salesman. He says to his mother in a truth-telling outburst: "Let's face it. As a human being I'm about C-. As a husband I'm about zilch. When Verity [the job press where he works] folds I'll fold with it and have to go on welfare." As Armstrong descends from the landing vehicle to the moon, mother and son watch vague

shadows moving on the screen and finally electronic letters proclaiming MAN IS ON THE MOON. Armstrong
tells Houston that it is easier to move around on the moon
than it was in simulations on earth, but at this point Rabbit, an earthbound creature borne down by familiar
earthly concerns, turns abruptly to his mother and speaks
about the loss of his wife: "I don't know, Mom. I know it's
happened, but I don't feel anything yet."

The epigraph of the novel's final section is a portion of
the conversation between Aldrin and Armstrong as Armstrong descends the ladder from the landing vehicle to the
moon's surface. Aldrin talks him down the ladder: "You're
lined up on the platform. Put your left foot to the right a
little bit. O.K., that's good. More left. Good." And Armstrong at last replies: "O.K., Houston, I'm on the porch."
Updike appears to mean the conversation to apply to
Rabbit's situation at the end of the novel: like Armstrong
he is on the porch, the final rung of the ladder, about to
take the last step—but whereas Armstrong's movement
will bring him to the surface of the mysterious moon,
Rabbit's, we are to understand, brings him more deeply
into his own mysterious life. Earlier in the novel, Jill, a
young girl who moves in with Rabbit to replace his absent
wife, tells him: "Because of the competitive American
context, you've had to convert everything into action too
rapidly. Your life has no reflective content; it's all instinct,
and when your instincts let you down, you have nothing
to trust." This appears to be Updike's view of Rabbit as
well: he needs to sink more into himself, becoming less an
instinctive, fleeing "Rabbit" and more the interior, reflective man. At the novel's end Rabbit seems to be in position
for this "redux," this (as Updike explains with a diction-
ary definition at the beginning of the novel) return to
health after disease. He is reunited with his wife in the
setting of a motel bed and they tentatively explore the
grounds of a new relationship, a relationship for Rabbit

based on the admission of an interior state that has not
marked his life to this point: guilt. Rabbit tells his wife:

> "I feel so guilty."
> "About what?"
> "About everything."
> "Relax. Not everything is your fault."
> "I can't accept that."

Whereas Armstrong is prepared to step down to the unknown moon, Harry Angstrom's journey seems to lead
more deeply into himself through the experience of ancient human emotion. Appropriately, in the novel's final
scene he fits himself to his wife's familiar body before they
fall asleep, and Updike describes "the space they are in"—
in pointed contrast to the outer space of *Apollo 11*—as an
intensely human "burrow" that for them "becomes all interior space."

In his poem "Moon Landing," W.H. Auden salutes
Apollo 11 as a "grand gesture" but then asks: "But what
does it period? What does it osse?" His answer, not unlike
that which emerges from *Rabbit Redux*, is that it "periods" very little in relation to unlifted, unaltered human
nature. The poem goes on to remark:

> We were always adroiter
>   with objects than lives, and more facile
>   at courage than kindness: from the moment
>
> the first flint was flaked this landing was merely
> a matter of time. But our selves, like Adam's,
>   still don't fit us exactly, modern
>   only in this—our lack of decorum.

Bellow's *Mr. Sammler's Planet* is similarly concerned
with a modern lack of earthly decorum, and like Updike's
novel it employs the triumphs and future possibilities of

space exploration in ironic counterpoint to the messy yet human concerns of the earthbound. Believing her father— an old and nearly blind Polish Jew living in New York of the late 1960s—at work on a definitive study of H. G. Wells, Sammler's daughter appropriates a manuscript on *The Future of the Moon* written by an Indian scientist, Dr. Govinda Lal. Because of Wells's speculations on the moon, circa 1900, the daughter assumes Sammler will be interested in the manuscript, as he is, though not because of the connection with Wells. The first sentence poses a question that intrigues him, "How long will this earth remain the only home of Man?", and throughout the novel he returns to it, pondering whether indeed it might be time, given an accumulation of problems, to depart from the planet.

Sammler's first impression of Lal's work is that it merits serious attention. The subject, technical speculation on requirements for colonization of the moon, is extreme and perhaps foolish but interesting nonetheless. Lal "brought news" of all the "technological expertise and investment and complex organization required for visiting Mars, Venus, the moon." Furthermore, the imaginative range of the book cannot be dismissed; as Sammler puts it, "it was perhaps for the same human activities that have shut us up like this to let us out again. The powers that had made the earth too small could free us from confinement." For Sammler the thought of technological escape from a world made too small by technology becomes a question to muse about and at last to measure against the hard human requirements of staying put amid increasing chaos.

At times Sammler wonders if the kind of moon colonization envisioned by Lal might not, by draining off population, make the planet a more habitable place for growing numbers caught up in a passion for wholeness, people who will acknowledge no limits on their lives, who want everything and will tolerate nothing less. At other times, his mood darker, Sammler notes that earth is a grave, and

that human life is lent to it by its elements and must be
returned; there is a time "when the simple elements seem
to long for release from the complicated forms of life,
when every element of every cell said, 'Enough!' " The
earth is both our mother and our burial ground so there is
no wonder the "human spirit wished to leave. Leave this
prolific valley. Leave also this great tomb."

Other characters also bring space exploration into the
story, thrusting it into Sammler's mind together with the
subject of Lal's manuscript. Wallace Gruner, the feckless
son of Sammler's patron and friend Dr. Elya Gruner, tells
him that the airlines are already taking reservations for
moon excursions: "Hundreds of thousands of people
want to go. Also to Mars and Venus, jumping off from the
moon." When Wallace asks if Sammler is interested in
such a trip, the old man indicates that his travelling days
are over because of age. More than that, he is "content to
sit here on the West Side, and watch, and admire these
gorgeous Faustian departures for the other worlds."

During a meeting between Lal and Sammler, the Indian
scholar explains that he hopes to publish his work by the
time of the first moon landing. He envisions a hoard of
bad paperbacks coming out, confusing the public about a
serious subject; his book would be the corrective. Lal believes that as far as Washington is concerned, and perhaps
the general public as well, a moon expedition is simply
superb show business; for the engineers that work on the
project it is a vast opportunity but still not something of
high theoretical value. Nevertheless, Lal insists that despite the relatively trivial attitudes at work in moon exploration, the feats cause something serious to happen within
society. He tells Sammler: "The soul most certainly feels
the grandeur of this achievement. . . . I believe the soul
feels it, and therefore it is a necessity." When Lal wonders
if Sammler agrees that space exploration is a necessity, the
old man offers a qualified yes: "Well, why not? Up to a
point, yes. Although I don't think it can be rationally jus-

tified." But Lal objects that space exploration is a rational necessity even if it cannot be rationally justified. Given the multitudes that cram the earth, Lal argues, we simply cannot manage with a single planet; we have to overflow into the universe. Psychologically, we must also understand that to fail to accept the opportunity that space offers would make the earth seem more and more a prison.

Sammler finds himself in general sympathy with Lal's view of the metaphysical need for space travel even though he continues to insist that such ventures may not be totally sensible given a world in which much remains to be done. He tells the Indian scholar:

> As an engineering project, colonizing outer space, except for the curiousity, the ingenuity of the thing, is of little real interest to me. Of course the drive, the will to organize this scientific expedition must be one of those irrational necessities that make up life—this life we think we can understand. So I suppose we must jump off, because it is our human fate to do so. If it were a rational matter, then it would be rational to have justice on this planet first. Then, when we had an earth of saints, and our hearts were set upon the moon, we could get in our machines and rise up.

But what makes the deepest impression on Sammler—and the view that finally is set in juxtaposition to speculations about space travel—is the willingness of many, saints or not, not to rise up, not to give way to the irrational necessities that make up life but to remain in earth-bound anxiety and perform their duties. Despite what Sammler diagnoses as the "fever of originality that grips modern man, the troublesome idea of the uniqueness of the soul," there also persists what he sees as a "thick sense of what is normal for human life." Duties are observed, there is discipline, drill, regularity, the assumption of responsibility and a regard for order—all of which remains a great mystery for such a restless creature as man.

The novel ends with Sammler standing over the corpse of his friend Dr. Gruner in a hospital post-mortem room and offering a hymn of celebration to a life lived in the mysterious pursuit of duty, a life thus ennobled. Unlike his son Wallace, Gruner had not signed on for space travel; unlike Lal, he had not given thought to leaving the earth behind. Instead, for reasons Sammler does not pretend to penetrate, he simply did his job, meeting life in its full earthly confusion. Says Sammler: "He was aware that he must meet, and he did meet—through all the confusion and degraded clowning of this life through which we are speeding—he did meet the terms of his contract. The terms which, in his inmost heart, each man knows. As I know mine. As all know." Earth is for Sammler, as it was for Gruner, finally sufficient. It still provides a landscape in which lives can fulfill a capacity to become human.

Another and more direct use of a return-to-earth conception of space exploration was as a transcendent experience through which earthly problems are seen with sudden clarity and consequently take on fresh urgency. In this use of space we are not so much made aware of an ironic gap between moon landings and earthly strivings as urged to consider earth from the vantage point of space, recognize it as our fragile home, and bring a once-and-for-all dedication to solving its problems. From such a perspective, earth is spaceship earth and we are all astronauts. Archibald MacLeish memorably established this way of thinking when he wrote in the *New York Times* after the moon-orbiting flight of *Apollo 8* (and in 1978 published in his book *Riders on the Earth*) that it might now be possible, man having "seen the whole earth in the vast void as even Dante never dreamed of seeing it," for man to "discover what he really is." MacLeish added, in a sentence frequently quoted: "To see the earth as we now see it, small and blue and beautiful in that eternal silence where it floats, is to see ourselves as riders on the earth together, brothers on that bright loveliness in the unending night— brothers who *see* now they are truly brothers."

The hero of Robert Lipsyte's novel *Liberty Two* (1974), a former astronaut named Charles Rice, has an experience on the moon along the lines suggested by MacLeish. While on the moon's surface Rice transmits a jeremiad to earth: "Tonight I have seen the earth plain. I have seen the purposelessness, the decay, the corruption. I have seen the murderous vanity that hurls us into space." The transmission is cut off, but when Rice returns to earth, dismissed by NASA and known as the mad moon man, he paints a school bus silver, christens it Liberty Two, and sets off through the country proclaiming a second American Revolution. What Rice has in mind is hazy but it has something to do with ridding the country of corruption and starting over in light of his vision of earth from the distance of space. Rice continually refers to the cleansing experience of seeing earth "plain" and thus recognizing for the first time "all the corruption, all the enslavement, the manipulation, the forgeries and false trappings" and resolving to do something about them. He tells his audiences from atop the silver bus: "We have to flush out our minds and our homes and our rivers and our governments."

The story of Rice's revolution is told by Cable, a journalist who joins Rice as a press secretary but in fact is in the employ of a secret organization known as The Center. The Center wants Rice stopped, presumably because he threatens the interests of its mysterious backer Douglas Clune in an unchanged America. Cable is gradually drawn to Rice and finally overtaken by his vision of radical change. By the end of the book Rice has attracted a vast army of followers and is preparing to fly by helicopter to the Los Angeles Coliseum to give a speech that will be carried on national television. Cable finally realizes that

Rice will be assassinated by The Center since it is clear that he cannot be controlled. Cable prevents one assassination attempt but finally Rice's helicopter is blown up on its flight to the Coliseum.

In a closing scene Cable sets off to expose The Center and its involvement in the former astronaut's death. And since he uses Rice's own visionary language at the end ("There'll be a way. There's always a way") the reader apparently is to believe that Cable may also take up Rice's revolutionary task. One of the weaknesses of the novel, however, is that it is unclear how we are to take Rice, and consequently how we are to understand Cable's use of his language. Is Rice a demagogue, manipulating the masses with shrewd media techniques, or a saintly visionary? Lipsyte does not seem quite certain himself, though presumably the reader is to accept Rice's defense of himself as one who wishes to "cut strings, not to pull them" as an honest sentiment.

In the work of Anne Morrow Lindbergh the use of the return-to-earth theme turns on an awareness of the ecological interdependence of earth rather than a vision of human corruption and mismanagement. In *Earth Shine* (1969), a prose meditation that followed her viewing of the launch of *Apollo 8*, she joined a new essay, "The Heron and the Astronaut," with an account of a trip to Africa, "Immersion in Life," originally published in 1966. The reason for linking two seemingly dissimilar essays, she explains, is that space exploration has drawn fresh attention to earth and it was in Africa that man took the first evolutionary steps that led him to the moon and the opportunity to view earth from space.

In the first essay, after describing the mechanical wonders of the Kennedy Space Station and the awesome rocket launch, Mrs. Lindbergh tells how she and her family spent the rest of their time in the wildlife sanctuary maintained by NASA on Cape Canaveral. "Instinctively," she writes, the space shot caused them to "want to touch earth again, to drench ourselves in nature," and so they seek out the natural wonders of 50,000 wild acres. Instead of the giant gray-and-white Vehicle Assembly Building on the horizon, her eyes now "pick up white herons, standing in ditches, poised motionless for prey." In the last part of the essay, *Apollo 8* successfully back to earth, Mrs. Lindbergh asks what it all means, and answers: "Along with a new sense of earth's smallness, a fragile, shining ball floating in space, we have a new sense of earth's richness and beauty, marbled with brown continents and blue seas and swathed in dazzling clouds—the only spot of color in a black and gray universe." Through the astronauts, she concludes, "we have seen more clearly than ever before this precious earth essence that must be preserved," an essence she suggests we call "Earth Shine."

As might be expected, popular novelists were drawn more centrally to space exploration that serious writers, using it not for the ironic counterpoint of Updike or Bellow but as direct subject. But they too tended to work within a broad return-to-earth framework, finding in space exploration fresh backgrounds for illustrating some of the familiar earthly preoccupations of thriller fiction. *Liberty Two* belongs partly in this camp, but a pure example of the type is James Blumgarten's *The Astronaut* (1974), a novel that draws on the endless fascination with strange death—in this instance the death of an astronaut who fails to return from space, his capsule turned into an orbiting coffin.

Franklin Weiss, a TV news reporter, covered the 1963 Mercury flight in which astronaut Tom Beckwith was incinerated while attempting re-entry into earth's atmosphere, his remains still circling the planet. Just before the *Apollo 11* moon landing his network decides on a round-up documentary on the space program and Weiss is sent to Florida to interview Beckwith's widow. An affair follows, the widow at loose ends since her husband's death and filling the time with sex; Weiss himself is under the strain of a failing marriage and filled with self-loathing that causes him to draw invidious comparisons with a heroic figure like Beckwith. But from the widow Weiss gets hints of something wrong, untold, about the Beckwith story—and the reader gets similar hints from italicized sections spaced throughout the novel giving Beckwith's thoughts during his fatal flight.

Weiss goes about the country seeing people who knew Beckwith, finally learning that the astronaut as a young man was in love with a girl who drowned and was lost at sea in a sailing accident. Beckwith felt responsible and never forgot the accident. A NASA radio technician who had contact with Beckwith at the end tells Weiss the astronaut failed to fire his rockets for re-entry and told radio trackers he did not want to return to earth. Beckwith's final moments are dramatized, the ground asking "Tom—why?" and Beckwith answering: "There's nothing to come back to." He longs only to join his former girl friend in death. The truth about her husband's death out, Mrs. Beckwith plays a recording for Weiss that the astronaut left her in which he says the only reason he got into the space program was "because the further I get from this crappy world the happier I am." The final lines of the novel belong to Weiss: " . . . I can't . . . look up at the sky. Because *he's* there, up beyond the sky. A mummy in a hermetically sealed tomb, 53 orbits a day. . . . Sooner or later, they tell me, the laws of physics will bring him down. In about a year, they tell me."

Blumgarten's thriller draws not only on the grim possibility of dead astronauts left in space but on an exposé mentality that *knows* the astronauts could not have been as antiseptically good as NASA publicity made them out. Similarly, Danny Stuart, the astronaut commander of a space station in Martin Caidin's *The Cape* (1971), has an affair with a young woman from Cape Canaveral, gets her pregnant, and then becomes involved in a botched abortion handled through a local hoodlum. But at the novel's end Stuart, humanly flawed but still noble, is back with his wife who in turn has become friendly with the woman who suffered the abortion. This bit of astronaut revelation, however, is only a sub-plot of Caidin's thriller. The main story deals with Russian sabatogue, in this case directed to the Saturn launch of America's first space station. There is an epic explosion in the Vehicle Assembly Building that kills thousands, but Ray Curtis, the novel's central figure and Director of Manned Launch Operations, decides to proceed with the launch despite the threat of more violence. At the last moment a Russian spy, a long-time engineer in the space program, is killed by another engineer and double agent while trying to activate a bomb that would have destroyed the space station and the astronauts after the launch.

The Cape deals with space engineers more than astronauts and is filled with presumably authentic detail of space-launch technology. The engineers, save for the spy in the lot, are shown to be brilliant, dedicated, hardworking types, with Curtis as the prototype. The book also devotes considerable attention to the Cape Canaveral area, which is shown as flashy, hard-driving, with an excessive number of divorces and high liquor consumption and drug addiction among the young. The impression the book gives is that the Cape area reflects in often tawdry ways the glitter and tension of the space program.

The familiar U.S.-Russian rivalry at work in Caidin's novel clearly offers special possibilities for thriller fiction when applied to space exploration. To date no one has exploited those possibilities quite like Allen Drury in *The Throne of Saturn* (1971); while Caidin keeps his spy story on the ground, Drury goes to the moon for his confrontation with the Russians. For nearly 600 pages he details the rise, fall, and rise again of *Planetary Fleet One*, a four-man, eighteen-month mission to Mars that takes place sometime in the late 1970s. In a foreword Drury thanks various people associated with NASA for help in the six months of research devoted to the book, research that shows through the novel in great chunks of information about space technology and NASA politics.

But only the book's setting deals with space exploration. Its theme is a familiar one for Drury readers: the Cold War clash between hawks and doves, the realistic and the soft-minded. The Mars expedition is threatened at every step by liberal do-gooders who question the importance of the mission, demand that a black be a crew member, and pooh-pooh reports that the Russians plan an attack on the Americans in space so they can be first to land on Mars. Colonel Connie Trasker, the heroic commander of *Planetary Fleet One*, insists on arming the space vehicle to repel attacks, but liberals in government and the media persuade the President that the act would destroy détente, and finally the mission goes unarmed but with Trasker and his crew carrying pistols.

After 400 pages of delays, controversies, and sabotage, the mission is launched. But even then the opposition is far from silenced. Drury writes, characteristically: "A sour, sad, spiteful effluvia rose from the world in the wake of the beautiful launches. Those who created it had been momentarily silenced but it did not take them long to find full voice again. In their consistent attacks from the beginning upon the mission they had finally managed to besmirch space, perhaps the last bright jewel in America's crown; and their vindictive caterwaulings . . . still howled up from Earth and followed Planetary Fleet One, relentless, where it went." The Mars flight calls for a moon orbit and landing on the way. While on the moon Trasker and a fellow astronaut suddenly lose radio contact with Houston; soon thereafter they encounter a Russian astronaut who means to cut their pressure suits, presumably leaving the world to believe that two American astronauts had foolishly ripped their suits on moon rocks. But after a struggle in which the American astronaut is fatally wounded, Trasker manages to kill the Russian and leave the moon in the landing vehicle. In the hovering spacecraft, meanwhile, another drama is taking place. The black astronaut, angry and resentful of his white colleagues, pulls a gun on his partner, presumably meaning to kill him and then take refuge with the Russian astronauts who he assumes will welcome him as a black man. There is a shootout in which the black is killed and the white badly wounded. When Trasker returns to the spacecraft he takes control of the mission, manages to ram the Russian spacecraft that is armed and ready to fire on the Americans, and then with his wounded friend sends *Planetary Fleet One* heading back to earth.

During a Congressional investigation of the moon violence the liberal camp refuses to believe Trasker's account of what took place. But at length the President sides with Trasker and announces that the second Mars mission will be armed and Trasker will command it. The book ends with the launch of the renamed *Planetary Fleet Two*, outbound on the trip to Mars, and a lyric meditation by Drury on the courage of Trasker and his fellow astronauts in seeking out the secrets of God's universe.

In Drury's hands U.S.-Russian conflict set in space serves as a fresh setting for again articulating hard-line Cold War attitudes. Kurt Vonnegut turns the same subject into a brief, sensitive story suffused with humane and liberal feeling that readers of his fiction will likewise find familiar. "The Manned Missiles" consists of letters exchanged between a Russian and American father whose sons have died in a space accident. It is not entirely clear what has happened, whether the two spacecraft have simply collided or, more likely, the American spacecraft was sent up to destroy the Soviet spacecraft for military reasons. From what we learn about them through the letters, neither spaceman was a killer, but both were in the service of nationalistic forces they readily obeyed.

The fathers are filled with pride in their sons yet express

sympathy for each other. They are not bitter but painfully aware of loss. Neither fully understands what his son was doing in space, but the sons are sharply remembered and strong feeling flashes through the letters. The Russian says: "May the two men be the beginning of trust between peoples. May they mark the end of the time when science sent out good, brave young men hurtling to meet in death." He ends his letter with the phrase "I grasp your hand," a phrase the American repeats at the end of his own letter. The softly-stated irony of the story is that the two old men reach out to each other in a human way after their sons had reached out in the deadly ways of science and national interest.

At the same time that men were being sent to the moon and unmanned space machines to the nearer planets, there appeared in our popular culture a fascination with UFOs, communications from outer space, theories about ancient astronauts, and the like. It is tempting to see a connection between the two experiences, science's gradual removal of the mystery of the outer world turning man inward to the creation of space mysteries of the imagination. Just such a connection was offered by James Stupple to explain what he called the "beligerently antiscientific" nature of science fiction writing during the 1970s. The Viking expedition to Mars, Stupple remarked, finding no indication of life, was a great success from a scientific standpoint but destructive for science fiction. The mission told us that Mars was "hardly the kind of place to instill in us the 'wonder of space' for which science fiction has been so famous." The result is that the science fiction writer has "retreated ever more inward." Increasingly, he has given up the objective world of science for another "terra incognita where he is free to create involuted science-fictional fantasies born of his own private consciousness, or, if he still persists in holding on to some semblance of order, to the cold and meretricious realm of myth."

Wright Morris's *The Fork River Space Project* is not a
work of science fiction, but it portrays an interior world,
post Apollo and Viking, in which characters create or suc-
cumb to the sort of "involuted science-fictional fantasies"
that Stupple finds in current science fiction. Morris does
not directly link such private experience to the actual
events of space exploration, but his novel can be understood as revealing a mentality susceptible to private space
journeys in the wake of the engineering spectaculars of
space exploration, minds determined to get into orbits of
their own making. Kelcy, a writer of humor, and his
young wife Alice have a dry, domestic life on the Nebraska
plains overturned when they become involved with a
plumber named Lorbeer and a house painter called Dahlberg. Lorbeer and Dahlberg are the only inhabitants of
Fork River, a ghost town abandoned when struck by a
strange twister that sucked up a portion of the town and its
inhabitants, leaving a crater behind. On weekends, Lorbeer and Dahlberg run something called the Fork River
Space Project, attracting a curious few to the ghost town
for a slide-and-sound show presumably intended to prepare them for an eventual landing of an unidentified flying object in the crater.

Dahlberg says the purpose of the project is to "restore
awe" since "without awe we diminish, we trivialize, everything we touch." "In two thousand years," he adds, offering an analogy with the origins of Christianity, "this is
the first new beginning," but in the case of the space project a beginning in which "it is the *earth* that is resur-
rected." Kelcy is curious but cannot believe in the space
project; a sense of humor gets in the way. But Alice can.
She is drawn to Dahlberg, and Kelcy watches her drift
away, unwilling to stop her since he values her right to
freedom. "Some people are determined to get into orbit,"
he says. "Was it so unusual that one of them was my
wife?" But Kelcy is pained and disoriented by his loss, feel-

ing the "chill, impersonal winds of space blowing in my face."

At the novel's end Alice goes off with Dahlberg, presumably to wait for the landing party from space that will whisk them off to new beginnings. A few days later Kelcy drives out to Fork River but the novel stops short of revealing what he discovers. "When I rounded the curve of the tracks up ahead," Kelcy asks, "what would I find?" Instead of providing the answer, Morris reveals Kelcy's mind, a mind not out of sympathy with the orbiting fantasies of Lorbeer and Dahlberg but not eager to rush into orbit itself. "It wouldn't surprise me at all," Kelcy says, "to feel the earth tremble, or note, on the sky over the canyon, the turbulence of air like ripples on water. The sense of buoyancy, of unearthly lightness, I had already felt and welcomed." But Kelcy does not believe in "rushing what is bound to happen." He is inclined to wait for the future, whatever it is going to be, and in the meantime feel "affection and longing" for Fork River as a place resonant with a pioneer past rather than a launch pad into the future.

The Fork River Space Project may be, as one reviewer put it, a bit murky at the center, yet it is one of the more intriguing fictional responses to space exploration in that it portrays what appears to be one of its most paradoxical effects. As science reduces space to problems in engineering, earthbound man finds fascination in UFOs and the promise of mystical new beginnings associated with space. Kelcy tells his wife never to look at anything too closely. "Take UFOs. You know when the jig is up? The jig is up as soon as one is identified." But Alice is not inclined to look too closely; her gaze is on the awe of which Dahlberg speaks. The space she presumably seeks is inner, mystical, the space of belief as against the space of rockets, astronauts, and televised moon landings; at the same time, it is belief turned to imminent arrivals from outer space. Morris's strange and complex novel probes a return-to-earth response to space exploration in which characters retreat inward to private fantasy, yet fantasy aflame with visions of resurrection in space.

For many, the Apollo moon landings were a disappointment. They had hoped, as Vincent Cronin has suggested, "that the moon would yield surprises: not life, of course, but something positively wayward, different, even perhaps funny—if not *Finnegans Wake*, at least a scene therefrom." In a poem called "After the Moon Walk," Edward Field makes the same point. What we really wanted when men landed on the moon "was for strange creatures to seize them":

> We wanted them to take off their helmets
> and discover they could breathe,
> that science was wrong
> and there was air there.

But science was not wrong. The moon's only surprise, Cronin notes, was that it held no surprises. So it is perhaps out of disappointment at the predictability of our real space journeys that Dahlberg and Lorbeer and Alice turn in upon themselves, creating space fantasies equal to their imagination—and that may well be the ultimate sense, for the time being at least, in which we insist on thinking of space exploration in terms of a return to earthly concerns, as somehow a meaning to us.

5   Lots of Rocks

.

In an article on "The Moon Landing and Modern Poetry," Laurence Goldstein describes the contrast between
the triumphal manner in which poets hailed Lindbergh's
solo flight across the Atlantic and the "less gracious
treatment" accorded the *Apollo 11* moon landing. *The
Spirit of St. Louis,* an anthology of poems drawn from a
national competition and published in 1927, offered uniform praise of Lindbergh's achievement as, in the words
of the editor of the volume, Charles Vale, a "validation of
all the American folklore in which an independent spirit
overcomes the mortmain of things as they are, the status
quo." *Inside Outer Space,* on the other hand, an anthology of space poems edited by Robert Vas Dias and published in 1970, is dominated by a skeptical attitude toward
space flight and the kind of wry irony that appears in Edward Field's poem.*

The measure of the change is suggested by the work of
Babettte Deutsch, the only poet represented in both an-
thologies. In 1927, she celebrated Lindbergh as "Showing
to the mean heart and cruel mind/ Provinces undiscov-
ered, rich beyond imagination,/ Not to be defined." But

---

*Charles P. Boyle, in a study of some of the social effects of space
exploration, was struck by a general lack of interest in space on the part
of poets. "One of the most perplexing aspects of the exploration of
space," he wrote, "is its minimal influence on literature, especially
poetry." Although space exploration seemed to offer all the ingredients
of epic poetry, poets had responded only with "years of silence."

in "To the Moon, 1969," imagination is not enlarged by the journey of *Apollo 11* but narrowed, deadened. Is the arrived-upon moon, she wonders, "simply a planet that men have,/ almost casually,/ cheapened?" She concludes the poem with a grim statement of "what has happened" as a result of the moon landing:

> But, for a few, what has happened is the death
>   of a divine
>   Person, is a betrayal, is a piece of
> The cruelty that the Universe feeds
>   while displaying its glories.

Other poets in the space anthology construct a similar view of the moon landings as somehow defiling the moon or dimming its bright presence in man's imagination. May Swenson asks: "Dare we land upon a dream?" In a poem called "Aesthetics of the Moon," Jack Anderson evokes the moon as "so pure, so complete/-ly nothing/ it is the absolute/ work of art:/ unparaphraseable and self-contained." He then laments:

> To set foot on it
>   even once
>   is to corrupt it utterly

When poets turn their attention to the astronuats, their responses are divided at best. In a poem called "Letter," Paul Blackburn admires the professional "cool" displayed by John Glenn, but after hearing Glenn speak on television, "mouthing banalities like any/ politician," he wonders: "what/ kind of hero is that?" Although the space shot was "fine and exciting," he concludes:

> But I would not walk
> four blocks to see you ride
> up Fifth Ave. in an open car.

A central theme running through the anthology is the contrast between the barren moon and inviting earth. In

"Voyage to the Moon," William Dickey portrays the moon as "a nation of pure philosophy/ Without sin or absolution." "There is no romance there, no air being present/ To carry the sound of compliment." Jack Anderson summarizes the discovered moon in bleak detail:

> rocks   lots of rocks
> dust   lots of dust
> rocks and dust   lots everywhere
> quite a sight   but nothing like home
> you can take my word for that

In "Toward the Space Age," William Stafford lists the life-sustaining elements of earth that men must take with them into space:

> We must begin to catch hold of everything
> around us, for nobody knows what we
> may need. We have to carry along
> the air, even; and the weight we once
> thought a burden turns out to form
> the pulse of our life and the compass for our
>   brain.

Beyond such essential biological matters there are other earthly pleasures one would wish to import into space: wind, rain, and "stray adventures." Likewise, in "The Skeleton," Robert Creeley celebrates not the mechanical "shell going outward" in which the astronauts must live in space but the human frame they "come back to, down to,/ and then to be in/ themselves only, only skin."

The most important American poet associated with space exploration has been James Dickey. In *Sorties* (1971), a collection of journal entries, Dickey located the public attention given space exploration in the belief that here at last was a meaningful activity in a world of increasing trivia. "But what must be seen," he added, "is that this enormous and impressive 'step for mankind' is a *triumph* of the trivial." The comment appeared to mark a significant shift in Dickey's conception of space journeys. In a prose-poem written for *Life* magazine in 1968, "The Triumph of Apollo 7," he had celebrated the astronauts as poets who would open the way to fresh public awareness of the wonders of space. Because of the astronauts, he wrote, "the death-cold and blazing craters of the moon will think with us, and the waterless oceans of Mars;/ the glowing fogs of Venus will say what they are." The lines bear resemblance to Stanley Kunitz's eager embrace of the moon venture in "The Flight of Apollo," a poem appearing in another collection of space poetry, Robert Phillips's *Moonstruck: An Anthology of Lunar Poetry* (1974):

> I was a stranger on earth.
> Stepping on the moon, I begin
> the gay pilgrimage to new
> Jerusalems
> in foreign galaxies
> Heat, Cold. Craters of silence.
> The Sea of Tranquillity
> rolling on the shores of entropy.
> And, beyond,
> the intelligence of the stars.

But in a second poem on the Apollo missions, "For the First Manned Moon Orbit," Dickey portrayed the astronauts as figures who "float on nothing/ But procedure alone,/ Eating, sleeping like a man/ Deprived of the weight of his own/ And all humanity in the name/ Of a new life." And he ended the poem by describing the flight back from the pitted moon "Bombed-out by the universe" to the "blue planet steeped in its dream/ Of reality, its calculated vision shaking with/ The only love." The concluding sentiment recalls Robert Frost's union of earth and love in "Birches":

> I'd like to get away from earth awhile
> And then come back to it and begin over.

May no fate willfully misunderstand me
And half grant what I wish and snatch me
      away
Not to return. Earth's the right place for love:
I don't know where it's likely to go better.

In "The Moon Ground," a third poem for *Life* that appeared in a July 4, 1969, issue, Dickey once again drew attention away from space journeys and back to earth, the "Human Planet." And again he portrayed the astronauts in reduced terms; they are on the moon "to do one/ Thing only, and that is rock by rock to carry the moon to/take it/ Back." Rather than deliverers from the trivial, the astronauts, in the closing lines of the poem, simply "stare into the moon/ dust, the earth-blazing ground." "We bend," they say, "we pick up stones." Likewise, in a poem called "Exchanges" published in *The Atlantic* in 1970, Dickey evokes an awesome launch at Cape Canaveral in which as the rocket was "drawn moonward inch by inch" it seemed likely the "quality of life/ And death changed forever/ For better or worse." But his personal response to the moon venture, set out at the end of the poem, is far less grand:

> Nothing for me
> Was solved. I wandered the beach
> Mumbling to a dead poet
> In a key of A, looking for the rainbow
> Of oil, and the doomed
> Among the fish.

Allen Ginsberg struck a more strident note in relation to space exploration in "In a Moonlit Hermit's Cabin," a poem included in the Phillips anthology, when he noted that within the "hours of Man's first landing on the/ moon—/ One and Half Million starv'd in Biafra" and "Football players/ broadcast cornflakes." Ginsberg also scoffed at the nationalistic fervor of the moon-landing broadcasts during which "TV mentioned America as much as Man" and Walter Cronkite pronounced "Russia soundly beaten!" "What Comedy's this Epic!" Ginsberg proclaimed in response, an airy dismissal of the space program that echoed John Berryman's remark in his poem "Apollo 8" that "these events are for kids & selenographers." Finally, Ginsberg issued a mysterious warning for the triumphal astronauts: "Plant the flag and you're doomed!"

In *Between Time and Timbuktu* (1972), a "space fantasy" play drawn from the work of Kurt Vonnegut and broadcast on public television, a poet is sent into space after winning a jingle contest sponsored by Blast-Off Food, the space food of the astronauts. Television commentators express the hope that Stony Stevenson will provide more evocative descriptions of space than earlier astronauts like "Bud Williams," who portrayed Mars as looking exactly like his driveway back in Dallas. Stony's flight takes him through a time warp, scattering him in time and space and dropping him into various grim adventures; but as it turns out the poet adds nothing to the descriptions of the astronauts. When his space capsule is found in the Pacific Ocean it is empty except for a cryptic note that reads: "Everything was beautiful and nothing hurt."

As a poet, Alfred M. Worden does considerably better. The command-module pilot for *Apollo 15*, Worden flew the spacecraft in orbit while Irwin and Scott explored the lunar surface. According to Irwin's theory, astronauts in Worden's position, heavily occupied with duties, were less changed by space experience than those in positions that allowed more leisure. But Worden was affected enough to publish a small volume of space poems, *Hello Earth* (1974), three years after his moon flight and to join Irwin's evangelical organization. As the book's title suggests, the poems have at least as much to do with earth as space; earth is celebrated as "ethereal, beautiful" and, despite our

ambitious space journeys, a "shrouded orb" that "we
cannot escape."

Worden arranges the poems in a sequence that begins
with his training period as an astronaut, goes on to treat
his moon flight and space walk, and concludes with medi-
tations on the space program as a whole and the heroic
image of the astronauts. In "Oceans," a poem set just before his moon launch, he evokes the beauty of earth and
asks: "How can I leave this lovely place/ To venture forth
in outer space?" His answer is that the space journey may
in fact be a return to earth, a step toward a renewed sense of
"home":

> While I love the scene around
> My mind imagines, without bound,
> Why I feel the call to roam
> Could it be a Lunar flight
> Is one small step towards home?

As the spacecraft hurtles into orbit Worden feels relief that
"everything works"—but at the same time he experiences
that sense of diminishment felt by other astronauts in
space, that sense that "Man is a fragile thing." In a poem
called "Perspective," set during the orbital flight, Worden
returns to the idea that the point of the moon trip is somehow to return to earth. He asks: "What value is this flight/
In a hostile ocean to an alien shore?" What can mankind
"learn" from the encounter with the dead moon? The only
possible answer comes to him when the "lunar disc slides
by the window" and then "earth drifts into sight." He
realizes that "Of all I can see or imagine,/ This is the most
beautiful," and he concludes the poem:

> Now I know why I'm here:
> Not for a closer look at the moon,
> But to look back
> At our home
> The earth.

Far out in space, in a poem called "240,000 Miles from Home," Worden again questions the point of the moon journey. "Why climb this hill?" he asks. The answer is that there are things to learn about earth and other planets, but what he chooses to emphasize is a moment of spiritual insight:

> One thing becomes clear
> When floating
> 240,000 miles from home—
> God did it all.

In subsequent poems, however, Worden does not return to whatever spiritual awareness he experienced during the flight. What occupies him instead is the contrast between earth and the moon. The moon reveals "no sign of healing, or love, or care, or compassion"—and this is the real instruction it offers beyond the scientific matters of "age and geology,/ planets and solar puzzles." The moon instructs him on the uniquely precious gift of earthly "life, else we end up like her." In the title poem, "Hello Earth," Worden adds about earth that "It's clear you are a spaceship/ And must do with what you've got."

In "Apollo Lost," a poem that offers justification for the space program, Worden responds to complaints that money would better have been spent on earth's needy with the thought—none too clear—that the program somehow brings them benefit:

> Say to me, we need the money
> Just to feed the poor, and more—
> And I'll say to you that's funny
> It's for them that we explore.

The book's final poem, "What Are Heroes?", celebrates the astronauts' bravery and joy in their work while noting as well their frequent disregard "of those at home who weep." Similarly, the poem suggests a tension between a devotion to skilled performance in space and the need,

once that performance is past, for new goals that satisfy an
awakened concern with earth. Worden writes:

> Magnificent performance on lunar surface
> Belies my need of an earthly purpose.

A passage in John Updike's *Rabbit Redux*, mentioned
earlier, describes workingmen drinking along a bar while
watching the flight of *Apollo 11* on television and feeling
unlifted themselves. The moon flight, awesome as it may
be, has no bearing on their lives; in relation to their very
earthbound lives, it hardly seems real. Likewise, when
Harry Angstrom hears news about space on television it
strikes him as "all about emptiness." The denial of space
implied in these responses, the denial of its reality in light
of personal lives, appears again—though in a more sophisticated formulation—in a lengthy Updike poem published in 1982. "The Moons of Jupiter" is a meditation on
the planet and its satellites insired by the dramatic photos
returned by Voyager, that "cloned gawker/ sent spinning
through symptotic skies/ and wildly televising back celestial news"—news, Updike pointedly adds, of threatening
space objects that "guides us to the brink of the bearable."

Updike considers in turn Jupiter's moons, Callisto,
Ganymede, Europa, and Io, reporting some of their sa-
lient features but finding in each some suggestive parallel
with familiar earthly experience. Callisto's pocked, ancient ice frozen four billion years ago is a terrain of "un-
forgiven wrongs and hurts preserved," of "the bad review,
the lightly administered snub," in which "All this cold
gloom keep jagged edges fresh/ as yesterday." Conversely,
Europa is still and smooth because "meteors here/ fell on
young flesh and left scars/ no deeper than birthmarks,"
suggesting the human world of accomplishment and
success:

> Around us glares the illusion of success:
> social polish, adequate performance,

> accreditations, memberships, applause,
> and mutual overlookings melt together
> to form one vast acceptance that make us
>   blind.

In the poem's final section Updike draws attention to the "forgotten witness" of the moons, Jupiter itself, and once again the celestial news relayed by Voyager inspires a return to a more familiar world, to a way of coping with the news by relating it to ordinary human experience. Confronting the reality of the planet, the poem suggests, is like the experience of ascending to the sixtieth floor of a building and there, "enormity" suddenly dawning, "the winds of space shining around us," sensing our narrow place in the universe in which we are no more than "beam walkers treading a hand's-breath of steel." In our vulnerability we are acutely aware of the planet's fearsome potential, its threat of crushing weight; our response, our quite understandable human response when faced with the fierce disclosures of space exploration, is to insist to ourselves that they cannot be real:

> Striated by slow-motion tumult
> and lowering like a cloud, the planet turns,
> vast ball, annihilating *other*,
> epitome of ocean, mountain, cityscape
> whose mass would crush us were we once
> to stop the inward chant, *This is not real.*

It is all real, of course. The cloned gawker has brought us incontrovertible celestial news. One way of contending with space revelations that may seem nearly unbearable ("vast ball, annihilating *other*") is to recast them in earthly terms or, finally, if only in an inward chant of personal resistance, deny them altogether. Like other American poets who have written about space, Updike in "The Moons of Jupiter" portrays space realities as harsh and threatening. He sounds much like Adrienne Rich who, in a 1980 poem called "The Spirit of Place," remarks that the constellations in the night sky all "look violent to me/ as a pogrom on Christmas Eve in some old country." And like other poets he turns away from those chill realities to evoke the world of ordinary—and for that reason comforting—human reality, appearing to agree with Rich when she says "I want our own earth/ not the satellites, our/ world as it is/ if not as it might be."

6   Visit Earth

George Held, writing in a special 1979 issue of *Michigan Quarterly Review* devoted to "The Moon Landing and Its Aftermath," was disturbed by the caution that novelists like Updike, Bellow, and Mailer brought to their literary treatments of space exploration. He found that they approached the subject from a "socially conservative position" rather than from "progressive attitudes"; they dealt with space only in "outmoded literary terms." He concluded that "these novelists, as well as most other literary intellectuals, have thus far resisted coming to terms with Armstrong's achievement as it manifests the power and sophistication of space technology and as it promises to affect the future of mankind. As men writing on the moon, these American novelists have yet to bring enough imaginative energy to the idea of man on the moon."

Whether novelists were as deficient in their treatments of space as Held maintained is, at least, arguable. But whatever the proper judgment on novelists, it seems clear enough that of those who wrote about space exploration in a serious vein it was journalists (including, in Mailer's case, a novelist on journalistic assignment) who brought to the subject the most verbal energy and provided the richest and most satisfying accounts. Perhaps it is always true that journalists give us our first and most energetic accounts of new experiences whereas the more osmotic forms of fiction and poetry require the passage of time before finally investing experience with symbolic and mythic resonance. In the long run, art-speech, as D. H. Lawrence told us, may be the only truth, but in the short run it is journalism that brings us news of the world—and with space exploration it often brought the news with insight and engaging style.

I have in mind here journalism of a particular sort—not the journalism of the daily newspaper or the evening telecast but book-length journalism by writers able to devote themselves to space exploration over extended periods of time. Some of the books belong in the category of "old" journalism; others were examples of the "new," and essentially literary, journalism that flourished in the 1960s and 1970s. Such works gave us lively accounts of the technological and scientific questions at stake in space exploration. They helped bring the astronauts to life as individual figures as well as skilled technicians. They told us something of the earthbound collection of engineers and scientists who worked behind the scenes to create space spectaculars and assess their results.

More than novelists and poets and even the astronauts themselves, journalists portrayed space exploration not only in light of what it revealed about earth but as an awesome and potentially transforming adventure into the unknown. In her book on the early years of the space program, the Italian journalist Oriana Fallaci comes to deeply admire the Mercury astronauts because they seem to her men "full of tomorrow," men turned not to the past but to whatever the future may bring. But the difference, finally, between space accounts by journalists and other writers may be slight. If journalists gave somewhat more attention to the futuristic aspects of space exploration than did others, they nevertheless framed their work within a similar return-to-earth conception of space journeys. They too, finally, portrayed the deepest meaning of space exploration as a meaning to us, the earthbound.

Henry S. F. Cooper, Jr., has written regularly about space matters for *The New Yorker*. His work for the magazine has subsequently appeared in five books that, taken together, comprise the most sustained and illuminating reporting available about the age of space.* Cooper has focused his work, however, on aspects of space that were given little or no treatment in day-to-day journalism, with the result that there is considerable freshness in his accounts, a view of space exploration from a slightly new angle.

For example, *Apollo on the Moon* (1969) deals with what the *Apollo 11* astronauts were likely to find on the moon, Cooper explaining that the book should be read "in the manner of someone reading the script of a play, complete with descriptions of scenery and instructions, before he goes to see it." *Moon Rocks* (1970) treats the anticipation and scientific questioning with which geologists and other scientists awaited the moon rocks brought to earth by *Apollo 11*. In *Thirteen: The Flight that Failed* (1973), Cooper recreates the hazardous journey of *Apollo 13* in which an in-flight explosion caused the command group on earth to bring the space vehicle back, and in so doing to create new procedures from scratch. *A House in Space* (1976) describes three Skylab flights in which astronauts, unlike those who flew in the Apollo program, had the experience of actually living in space in a vehicle thirty-three times larger than an Apollo spacecraft. Cooper's most recent book, *The Search for Life on Mars* (1980), examines the Viking landings on the red planet and the complex efforts of scientists to find life on the planet.

The first three books stress the technological and scientific issues involved in space exploration rather than the individual achievements and personalities of the astronauts who flew the missions. Cooper draws particular attention to the ground personnel, the engineers and the scientists, who remained largely faceless in most reporting about the space program. In *A House in Space* he turns the

*A sixth book, *Saturn*, is scheduled for publication at this writing and two long accounts of the space shuttle program have appeared in *The New Yorker* (February 9 and 16, 1981).

focus on the astronauts, but once again his approach has a twist to it in that the Skylab astronauts, living in space, had more time to observe as they orbited through space and consequently provided much richer accounts of their experiences than did earlier astronauts.

Cooper does not shrink from giving the reader an abundance of technical detail about space exploration, but in *The New Yorker* tradition his work remains literate and readable. He also is able to endow his subjects with dramatic qualities that provide an engaging narrative spine for his books. In *Moon Rocks* there is the question of whether the rocks, upon investigation, will confirm or destroy scientific theories. Cooper personalizes the scientists engaged in the work and portrays their world as filled with as much drama as that of the astronauts; indeed, *Apollo 11* is described as a "flawless dramatic production" in which the astronauts were following a rigid script, whereas scientists had no script and consequently were deeply excited by whatever revelations the moon rocks would bring. In *Thirteen* the reader wonders how the damage will be repaired and the astronauts brought back to earth. The mission bore some resemblance to the sinking of the *Titanic* in that the unthinkable happened; but the spacecraft had the ultimate in redundancy built into it—a whole other vehicle, the landing craft—and ultimately this saved the day. The astronauts entered the LM for the trip back through space, but for the re-entry into earth's atmosphere they had to return to the space module with its heat shield and jettison the LM. The powering up of the module after it had been dead had never been done before, even in simulation, and entirely new procedures were developed on the spot by a brilliant cast of experts on the ground.

Although the Skylab flights experienced no comparable disaster in space, the story Cooper tells in *A House in Space* does not lack dramatic quality. The last of the three Skylab flights described in the book caused mission control in Houston endless problems. At first the reader thinks the third crew petty and mean-spirited compared to the other two; but then we learn that the third crew is rebelling against overwork and overcontrol from the ground. The crew members exert their individuality and humanity and in the end the reader comes to think them the most admirable crew, the crew that ignored excessively heavy work schedules in favor of simply looking out the window of the spacelab and that provided the fullest and most vivid descriptions yet given of space. "It was, somehow, typical of NASA," Cooper comments, "to send men off on a totally new sort of experience, and then overplan it to such an extent that they had no time to think about what they were experiencing—an important reason for sending human beings into space in the first place."

In *Moon Rocks*, Cooper observes that the scientists, "who had in effect explored the moon more thoroughly than any astronaut," had found little there that would cause anyone to return: "no life, no water, no atmosphere, and nothing of commercial value, such as major mineral deposits." As a result, a geologist at the Space Center in Houston had tacked up outside his office a large photograph of a pale blue earth rising above a bleak grey moonscape. Below the picture were the words "visit earth," causing Cooper to conclude that "perhaps men had to go to the moon before they could clarify their picture of their own planet." In Cooper's books as a whole space exploration is presented as an exciting scientific and technological venture into the future. Cooper offers no visionary predictions about the future of space exploration, preferring to pin his accounts to actual details (or in *Apollo on the Moon*, likely details) of the events he records; but there is in his work a strong sense that the new discoveries are fundamentally changing the terms of life on earth.

Nonetheless, a "visit earth" theme appears prominently in Cooper's reporting about space exploration. In *A House in Space* he remarks that if the third crew described in the book "were influenced by anything in space, it was not so much by being weightless or by floating upside down as simply by what they saw out the window; they preferred looking at the view to anything else they did in their free time." In contrast to the Apollo astronauts who portrayed earth as an oasis in space, the Skylab astronauts were struck by earth's barren quality; most of the time they were looking at oceans and deserts and snowfields and mountainous areas in which they could see no sign of life. "Not much of the earth is hospitable to man," they told mission control. "We don't occupy much of our world. We're crowded into small areas." Their fascination with looking at earth, Cooper says, drew the Skylab astronauts "into a new frame of mind. Much of what they saw they already knew, but actually *seeing* it gave it a crystal clarity." When they returned to earth many of them said they had been changed by their space experience. They had new ecological concerns or new humanitarian interests or simply a new feeling of insignificance based on the experience, as Cooper puts it, of seeing "how big earth is, and they think how short their stay is upon it, and what a small mark man has made on it."

In *The Search for Life on Mars*, Cooper recounts the story of the Viking landings on Mars in the late summer of 1976 and the effect of the mission within the scientific community on the question of the existence of life on the planet. As in his earlier works, Cooper brings to light an aspect of space exploration not widely reported in the daily press, or at least not reported in extensive detail—in this case, the scientific findings made possible by the Viking landings—and directs attention to the scientists working behind the scenes in laboratories and research centers. And once again he endows his story with considerable dramatic intensity. Will the landings, his story asks, document an age-old belief in the existence of life on Mars or will they reveal, as many scientists had come to feel, that the red planet is as lifeless as the moon?

Of all the planets in our solar system, aside from earth, Mars had long seemed to scientists the most likely place for the existence of life. During the 1960s and 70s, NASA dispatched four Mariner spacecraft to Mars on observation missions. During the same period the Soviet Union sent at least eight spacecraft to the planet. The Viking mission, with actual landings on Mars during which ingenious biological and chemical experiments would be conducted by remote control, was designed to either confirm or deny the possibility of life on the planet. The question of life elsewhere in the universe seemed to many the central issue facing mankind; the ramifications, for the scientific community as well as the popular imagination, were immense. Although no direct evidence existed for life elsewhere, there was considerable indirect evidence that suggested that extraterrestrial life must exist. If it did not, scientists were faced with what seemed to be the most perplexing question of all: why was it that the physical and chemical conditions that promoted life existed on earth and nowhere else?

The scientist widely associated with belief that life existed on Mars as well as elsewhere in the universe was Carl Sagan, and the first half of Cooper's book concentrates on the Cornell University astronomer's enthusiastic arguments for extraterrestrial life while also describing the preparations for the Viking landings. One of Sagan's colleagues said about him that he "desperately wants to find life someplace, anyplace—on Mars, on Titan, in the solar system or outside of it. In all the divergent things he does, that is the unifying thread." But other scientists involved in the Viking program were as doubtful as Sagan was hopeful. One of them rated the chances of finding life on Mars as "low—not quite zero, but very low." If life was not found on Mars, it might of course exist elsewhere; it also was possible that life might escape detection by Viking. But if life was found in the harsh environment of Mars, the discovery—as Cooper puts it—"would speak volumes about an abundance of life, including intelligent life, all over the universe."

The second part of the book follows the work of various scientists with the data returned to earth after the successful Viking landings. The test results turned out to be puzzling and contradictory, and Cooper describes the ups and downs of scientific interpretation with the unfolding drama of a complex mystery story. Finally, with the Viking research instruments shut down for good, NASA issued a cryptic statement: "Biologists have not reached any final conclusions about the presence or absence of life on Mars." The weight of evidence, however, suggested that Mars was lifeless, causing some scientists to wonder if the factors required for life were so numerous that "life on earth might, after all, be unique." One of those factors appeared to be the existence of an ocean that functioned as a "nursery of life"—and in our solar system only earth possessed oceans.

In the book's epilogue Cooper reports that now, the Viking experiments over, scientists show little interest in the question of life on Mars. There have been no follow-up missions to the planet, and interest in life beyond the solar system also seems on the wane. One of the Viking landers is still returning photographs from Mars, and will do so into the 1990s, and Cooper notes that if anything "should wander slowly enough across the blasted, desiccated Marsscape, we will know." But the clear implication of the story he tells is that it is very unlikely. The search for life on Mars seems only to turn us back to the existence of life on earth. "If Mars is barren," Cooper quotes a Viking scientist, "it will force us to take another look at Earth."

Cooper's books employ traditional journalistic forms. Oriana Fallaci's *If the Sun Dies* (1966), on the other hand, is a freewheeling, personal account (neither reportage nor fiction, she says, but a diary or an autobiography) of her experience with the space program at the end of the Mercury days and with preparations for the Apollo moon landings. The book takes the broad form of a dialogue between the journalist and her father about the importance and meaning of space exploration. Fallaci describes herself as a person belonging to the new generation and the new world while her father, an old world figure living on a quiet farm near Florence, represents the past, the unchanging. Her father, she says, "belongs to a generation firmly anchored to the Earth and the past; I belong to a generation facing a future of dizzy horizons and thirsty for new ideals." The book is the writer's effort to convince both herself (although she does not belong to her father's generation, she shares many of its feelings for the past) and her father that space exploration is not to be feared or viewed as prideful indulgence but embraced as a necessary leap into the future.

Fallaci visits the important centers of space activity, comes to know many astronauts and NASA officials, and witnesses rocket launches. Among the familiar figures appearing in her account are Wernher von Braun, Deke Slayton, Pete Conrad, Gordon Cooper, and Neil Armstrong; but special attention is given to a relatively unknown figure, the astronaut Theodore Freeman. For Fallaci, Freeman stands out from the other rational, obedient, prematurely aging astronauts. He almost seems an "astronaut by mistake," enthusiastic about bicycle riding, poetry, and painting as well as flying. Fallaci happily suspects that when NASA took him into the astronaut program they "wanted to have some fun or they didn't realize what a jewel they had."

Five months after their meeting, Freeman is killed in a freak airplane crash. Near the end of the book Fallaci describes his funeral, with the astronaut corps in attendance for the burial in Arlington National Cemetery. The astronauts show no emotion over the death, responding to Fallaci's questions about it with the flat remark that it could just as well have been one of them. Eventually, Fallaci comes to feel that the lack of response is not indifference but acceptance of death on the part of pilots as a natural part of their world. The astronauts now seem to her rich with life in the sense that only in the acceptance of death can life be lived to the full. At the same time they seem to her men "full of tomorrow" for they know that if one of them falls the others will carry on; for this reason, Fallaci notes, "it was useless to say prayers over a rocket that's going up" because regardless of what happened there would be other rockets going up.

This view of the astronauts—strong, at ease with death, fully alive, turned to the future—is finally what Fallaci sets against her father's feeling for the past and an unchanged earth. At one point, she addresses her father with such a conception of the astronauts: "I had grown to feel affection for them as well as respect, a sort of envy. And my affection for them came from having understood one important thing: that they were not, they are not, different from ourselves, Father, they *are* ourselves. They are ourselves who a century ago, two, three, centuries ago, left old Europe and went to seek new shores and new hopes. They are us moved to another address." In other words, the astronauts represent, for the present, the forward thrust of life, the enduring exploring spirit of man.

What the astronauts are exploring, of course, is the new world of space, but Fallaci suggests a connection between this world and the world of the past, the old world represented throughout the book by her father. At the beginning of the book she recounts a conversation with Ray Bradbury in which he described space exploration as a journey out to other suns that keeps life going if our own sun should die. We save ourselves, in other words, our history and our achievements on earth, by the journey into space. Bradbury tells her:

> Let us prepare ourselves to escape, to continue
> life and rebuild our cities on other planets: we

shall not long be of this Earth! And if we
really fear the darkness, if we really fight
against it, then, for the good of it, let us take
to our rockets, let us get well used to the great
cold and heat, the no water, the no oxygen
. . . let us go to the other solar system . . .
to wherever we manage to go, and let us forget
the Earth. Let us forget our solar system and
our body, the form it used to have, let us become no matter what . . . all that matters is
that somehow life should continue, and the
knowledge of what we were and what we did
and learned: the knowledge of Homer and
Michelangelo, of Galileo, Leonardo, Shakespeare, of Einstein! And the gift of life will
continue.

In the final lines of the book (as well as in its title) Fallaci returns to this view of space exploration as a means of
maintaining earthly life even in the absence of earth.
While walking with Bradbury in New York she sees a time
capsule, constructed to last until 6965, being lowered into
place. The capsule, Bradbury tells her, contains artifacts
of human civilization to 1965, the eve of flights to the
moon, so that men in the far future might know something of how we have lived. The time capsule returns Fallaci to the view Bradbury had suggested to her of space
exploration as a way of maintaining earthly life, and she is
filled with optimism. Through space exploration earthly
achievements will endure, even if our sun dies.

Like Fallaci's book, Norman Mailer's report on *Apollo
11, Of a Fire on the Moon* (1970), involves, as he says, a
"philosophical launch"—that is, an effort not simply to
report on space exploration but, through the medium of
personal journalism, to arrive at some evaluation of it that
at least satisfies the author. The task is a formidable one

given that "space matters," as Mailer admits, are "foreign
to him." The flight of *Apollo 11* is acknowledged as the
"hardest story of them all" in Mailer's varied career as a
novelist and journalist. The problem is that Mailer cannot actively participate in the technological triumph. He
cannot address an audience, join in a march, or get himself jailed as he did in *The Armies of the Night* and so
launch his philosophical quest from within personal experience. In *Of a Fire on the Moon* he is forced into the
uncomfortable role of observer of a wonderworld of engineering that does not yield to his casual credentials; he
must, like other outsiders, view the rocket launch from the
bleachers at Cape Canaveral and watch the moon landing
on television. Even the moon rock he eagerly inspects at
the book's end must be seen in a hermetically sealed glass
case and through a window with yet another hermetic
seal. "Is it possible," Hilton Kramer began a review of the
book, "to write *Moby-Dick* without ever having been to
sea?"

The astronauts prove an equally stubborn subject for
the journalist-philosopher. Their language is vacuous,
their personalities flat and reserved. Mailer finds in them
little that is distinctive, finally coming to believe that the
logic of the moon mission demanded that the men must be
as interchangeable as the parts of their machines. More
troubling is the lack of wonder or heroism the astronauts
exude. Mailer invokes them as "technicians and heroes,
robots and saints," but nothing helps him come to grips
with them. Although he insists that there is surely more to
them than meets the eye, more ambition or fear or nobil-
ity, Mailer cannot pierce their closed world. Of the NASA
hierarchy gathered for the moon launch, including many
of the earlier Mercury astronauts like John Glenn and
Deke Slayton, Mailer says they were "as closed to superfi-
cial penetration as a guild of Dutch burghers in the Seven-
teenth Century." He adds that the story of their internal
struggles during the years of the moon program "was

another of the great novels of the world which would
never be written."

Despite the difficulties posed by his subject, Mailer provides a good deal of detailed and illuminating information about *Apollo 11* and portrays a number of the people
involved in the flight (Neil Armstrong especially) with a
penetrating eye. But his deepest concern is always with
larger matters—with the philosophical quest to understand the meaning of the adventure in space. To this end
he relies on a solution that is a familiar one in his work:
the creation of dualisms; or as Richard Poirier has described the method, Mailer proceeds to "divide the material, argue the difference, reach a kind of stalemate, and
call it a 'mystery.' "

In *Of a Fire on the Moon*, Mailer ponders a number of
dualisms, all involving the possible meaning of the
voyage to the moon. It is, he wonders, "the noblest expression of the Twentieth Century or the quintessential
statement of our fundamental insanity"? In the flight of
Apollo 11 are we witness to "grandeur or madness," mystery revivified or technology run riot? On the deepest level,
Mailer's questioning turns theological. In the towering
Vehicle Assembly Building at Cape Canaveral he feels
himself in the "first cathedral of the age of technology."
He wonders whether the astronauts and their machines
are at the service of "celestial or satanic endeavors"? "Was
the Space Program admirable or abominable? Did God
voyage out for NASA, or was the Devil our line of sight to
the stars?"

In Mailer's work it is the questioning, the philosophical launch, that matters more than answers that are only
hinted at, arrivals that are never quite detailed. Nonetheless, in the book's last chapter Mailer attempts at least
some resolution of the dualisms with which he probes the
meaning of *Apollo 11*. He tells of a Labor Day gathering,
shortly after the moon landing, during which friends in
Provincetown half bury a worn-out Ford with elaborate

funeral ritual. Children paint the exposed part of the car while the adults drink; later a sculptor welds the car into an artifact that bears some resemblance to the moon-landing vehicle. The episode suggests an ironic contrast between frivolous earthly activity and the stirring feat of the moon landing. Mailer pointedly notes that the Pilgrims had first landed in Provincetown, and so it is the town that "was the beginning of America for Americans," but now there is merely "an immense quadrangle of motel" on the spot where the Pilgrims had "rowed an explorer's boat to shore."

But if American life and the landscape have become trivialized (and Mailer's own mood is flattened by his brooding in the book on his "marriage ending and a world in suffocation and a society in collapse") the moon voyage still touches the depths of his imagination. He turns from the mock funeral of the Ford to tell in the last pages about seeing a moon rock in Houston, an "object at last for his senses." Something about the rock inspires in him positive feelings about the venture into space. In the presence of the rock he experiences a "subtle lift of love" that brings him to "in some part applaud the feat and honor the astronauts." He concludes that we "probably had to explore into outer space," but the purpose of the exploration should be—through the experience of the "mystery of new discovery"—the reawakening of an older and non-mechanical view of life, one in which we are brought to "regard the world once again as poets, behold it as savages."

Thomas Werge has written that Mailer's accomplishment in *Of a Fire on the Moon* is that he places space exploration within a familiar context of nineteenth-century American literature in which God and Satan are envisioned as struggling over the soul of the nation. In this tradition America itself is seen as a voyage, an errand in the wilderness, that is either salvific or destructive; in drawing on the tradition, Werge observes, Mailer "echoes the ambivalence of the Puritans, of Edwards, and of the great American authors of the 19th century" over the inner meaning of American life. Mailer's philosophical launch, in other words, draws space exploration within a framework of interpretation that lies at the base of our literary imagination; the flight of *Apollo 11*, the newest of epic American journeys, is to be understood in light of the earliest and most commanding conception of ourselves, as a people engaged in an ancient spiritual drama. Similarly, Mailer's final affirmation of the moon flight involves a return to the past in that space exploration may cause us to rediscover a pretechnological consciousness, the consciousness of poets and savages, in which we live once again within the worlds of mystery and metaphor.

Tom Wolfe's approach to space exploration in *The Right Stuff* (1979) also draws the reader back—but back to the early days of the space age and to familiar human activity rather than to Mailer's religious rhetoric and primitive consciousness. The book recalls the period of rocket-plane testing that took place at Edwards Air Force Base in California after the Korean War and, subsequently, the selection and flights of the original seven Mercury astronauts. This is the era that established the approach and the attitudes that went into the more celebrated moon landings of the Apollo program. To understand this period, Wolfe suggests, is to understand the forces at work in later and more publicized space activities.

In Wolfe's view the foremost thing to understand about the first astronauts is that they were pilots—and pilots of a special sort: fighter pilots and test pilots. As such, they conceived themselves as a breed set apart; they were men who daily risked their lives in the most hazardous forms of flying. They were motivated not only by a passion for flying but by egos that knew few limits and by a vision of an illusive goal apparent only to those within the profession, a goal that Wolfe calls the Brotherhood of the Right Stuff.

The Brotherhood resembles a pyramid and young pilots begin climbing it at the beginning of their careers. There is nothing written down about the pyramid, nothing in the manuals, but the pilots know exactly what steps are required to reach the top; they know they must reveal to themselves and others that they possess the "right stuff" and so are eligible to rise to the next level of the pyramid, eventually moving through a seemingly infinite series of tests into the elite company of a few pilots at the very top.

The exact nature of the "right stuff" varies depending on the particular flying challenge at hand: landing on a carrier, combat flying, testing experimental planes. The only common denominator is the assumption that "a man should have the ability to go up in a hurtling piece of machinery and put his hide on the line and then have the moxie, the reflexes, the experience, the coolness, to pull it back in the last yawning moment—and then to go up again *the next day*, and the next day, and every next day." The only fear the pilots have is the fear of being left behind, for to be left behind at any point in the climb up the pyramid is to fail utterly, and so they push themselves to extraordinary feats of daring and bravado—and celebrate themselves and their violent profession with bouts of drinking, reckless driving, and womanizing.

Wolfe describes the world of the "fighter jocks" with great verve. But his subject is broader in that he wishes to show how this narrow and in many ways old-fashioned manly activity influenced, and in turn was influenced by, later space exploits. The shape of the flying pyramid constantly changes, but in the 1950s it was clear where the top was located and equally clear who the man at the top was. The place was Edwards Air Force Base and the man was a young Air Force officer named Chuck Yeager. At Edwards, Yeager flew experimental rocket planes, and in 1947 he had become the first man to break the sound barrier. He also flew rocket planes to the very edge of space. Although Yeager's feats were not widely known to the public, they were well known among pilots. Similarly, Yeager's style—laconic, unshakeably cool—set the style for all fighter jocks.

In the beginning, celebrated test pilots like Yeager had little interest in space flights. They thought the first space vehicles would be little more than artillery shells; there would be little for an astronaut to do but ride along, a passenger rather than a pilot. It seemed appropriate that the first occupant of an American spacecraft would be a chimpanzee, trained to perform in space and the subject of stress experiments. When Yeager was asked why he had not chosen to become an astronaut, he said: "I've been a pilot all my life, and there won't be any flying to do in Project Mercury." At the same time, Yeager and others thought that the rocket planes, genuine airplanes that were flown into space and flown back, offered more interesting possibilities for space flight than rocket-launched capsules. It was clear to Yeager and others, at any event, that when the seven Mercury astronauts were chosen they were not selected as the seven hottest pilots around, those at the top of the flying pyramid, for the reason that they would not be doing any flying in space.

But despite the reservations of the test pilots, the shape of the flying pyramid began to change with the selection of the Mercury astronauts. The reason had nothing to do with flying but with public response to the astronauts. They became celebrities of the first order; they were admired, lionized, courted. *Life* magazine purchased their exclusive stories; they were frequent guests at the White House; and far from least in the eyes of fighter jocks, they were the objects of heated attention from attractive young women. "From the very beginning," Wolfe notes, "this 'astronaut' business was just an unbelievable good deal." It also became clear in time that the government, feeling the pressure of Russian space success, would push the Mercury program rather than rocket planes as the quickest way to achieve the eventual goal of a moon landing.

With the outpouring of public attention after the first Mercury flights of Alan Shepard and John Glenn, the flying pyramid was permanently altered. The seven Mercury astronauts "had *become* the True Brotherhood. They were so dazzling you couldn't even see the erstwhile True Brethren of Edwards Air Force Base any longer." As they cut back on medical and scientific tests in space and insisted on more and more control of the capsules, the astronauts also grudgingly came to be recognized by the test pilots as true pilots. Because of their exalted position in the public mind, NASA brass tended to go along with the astronauts' demand that in some ways they *fly* the capsules. At length, the astronauts received what Wolfe maintains they wanted most of all, the thing that they could not be given by the public: "acceptance by their peers, their true brethren, as *test pilots* of the space age."

In Wolfe's account the Mercury astronauts adjust space exploration from a scientific and technological venture, spurred on by Cold War competition, into conventional earthly status competition within the limited world of fighter pilots and test pilots. This may or may not be an accurate interpretation of the astronauts and the Mercury program, but Wolfe's account is fully persuasive (and fully in accord with an astronaut book like Walter Cunningham's *The All-American Boys*) and has the overall effect of removing space exploration from grand thoughts about the new ocean of space, scientific discoveries, and radical changes in consciousness and replacing them with a compelling account of familiar earthly striving.

Wolfe's reductive treatment of the space program can be seen as well in his characterization of the astronauts. Rather than heroic figures, they appear, as they appear in their own accounts, as recognizably human types—vain, courageous, competitive, and no more virtuous than the next person. The public image of the Mercury astronauts as simple small-town churchgoers and dedicated family men was, Wolfe maintains, largely set by John Glenn.

The most articulate member of the group, Glenn gave the media the kind of pious pronouncements they wished and generally comported himself in a way that attracted attention—all of which struck the other astronauts as unbecoming a dedicated fighter jock. But Glenn more than the others sensed the transforming possibilities offered by astronaut life and was not shy in seeking them out. The exclusive *Life* contract for their stories also protected the astronauts from close inspection by the media, with the effect that the astronauts appeared to the public as modest, dedicated, well-scrubbed figures. Wolfe's account restores them to their proper role as self-serving, hard-living fighter jocks.

Wolfe's treatment of the astronauts' experiences in space also is heavy with homely return-to-earth qualities. We learn that Alan Shepard urgently needed to urinate as he waited for his launch in the first manned Mercury flight, and finally followed the instruction of mission control to urinate in his space suit. We are told that the astronauts' feelings at the moment of launch had nothing to do with their families or with prayers for safety but with fears of making mistakes that would make them look bad in the eyes of peers. And Wolfe maintains that the astronauts gave few notable descriptions of their space experience because the flights were simply confirmations of what they had been trained to expect in space. They had gone through all the procedures hundreds of times in realistic simulations; the tendency during flights, then, was to contrast the real experience with the simulator training, and often conclude that the latter was more rigorous. "Even if he had been ordered at that point to broadcast to the American people a detailed description of precisely what it felt like to be the first American riding a rocket in space," Wolfe says, referring to Shepard's first flight, "and even if he had had the leisure to do it, he could not possibly have expressed what he was feeling. For he was introducing the era of pre-created experience. His launching was an utterly novel event in American history, and yet he could feel none of its novelty."

Nothing, finally, could be more ironic. The novelty of the first manned American space flight cannot be felt because the preparations had destroyed all sense of novelty; the very point of the training had been to make all eventualities familiar. Consequently, the highest praise for this and other flights was to say they went just the way they were programmed. The effect of such irony for the reader—and the effect of Wolfe's book as a whole—is, once again, to strip space exploration of any sense of new-world mystery, any sense of an adventure into the unknown, and portray it simply as a new twist in very common earthly experience.

In Henry S. F. Cooper, Jr.'s reporting, with its emphasis on scientific and technological questions, space exploration can seem an exciting voyage of discovery. In Oriana Fallaci's book the astronauts are applauded as men turned to the future, men devoted to discovering new worlds that will enable us to continue the old. Although he draws on language and feeling rooted in the pretechnological past, Norman Mailer nevertheless labors to invest the moon flights with appropriate awe and mystery. But in Tom Wolfe's hands the heady world of space exploration is returned to earth with a vengeance and the reader catches few glimpses of the stars. This of course is not necessarily a bad thing; it may even mark an advance in our understanding of space exploration. It simply makes it difficult to think of the astronauts as men of tomorrow and space flights as epic expeditions into the future.

At the start of the Mercury program, Wolfe reports, several of the astronauts who were Navy officers got together in a motel room for a serious discussion of the venture for which they had just volunteered. But contrary to our expectation, what they "talked about was not space travel, the future of the galaxy, or even the problems of riding a rocket into earth orbit. No, they talked about a rather more urgent matter: what this Project Mercury might do to your Naval career." With such homely revelations *The Right Stuff* brings us right back where we started, back to earth and all-too-familiar human response.

7 Pretty Country

In 1957, at the beginning of the space age, E. B. White used the launch of the Russian *Sputnik 2* with a dog aboard as the occasion for a *New Yorker* interview with the garrulous ghost of his deceased dachshund, Fred. White reported in "Fred on Space" that the ex-dog found little of interest in the new marvel in the sky. About the grand discoveries likely to follow from the Russian dog's mission in space, Fred was distinctly skeptical. "If a dog is going to unlock any secrets," he remarked, "don't send him into space, let him smell what's going on right at home."

White pressed Fred on the matter of new knowledge by asking if he did not believe that man might at last learn the secret of the sun. Fred replied at length:

> No chance. Men have had hundreds of thousands of years to learn the secret of the sun, which is so simple every dog knows it. A dog knows enough to go lie down in the sun when he feels lazy. Does a man lie down in the sun? No, he blasts a dog off, with instruments to find out his blood pressure. You will note, too, that a dog never makes the mistake of lying in the hot sun right after a heavy meal. A dog lies in the sun early in the day, after a light breakfast, when the muscles need massaging by the gentle heat and the spirit craves the

> companionship of warmth, when the flies
> crawl on the warm, painted surfaces and the
> bugs crawl, and the day settles into its solemn
> strike, and the little bantam hen steals away
> into the blackberry bushes. That is the whole
> secret of the sun—to receive it willingly. What
> more is there to unlock?

From a dog's point of view, Fred insisted, journeys in space made no sense. The earth was enough. "No dog," he said, "would fritter away his time on earth with such tiresome tricks." Man's curiosity had finally led him into space whereas a dog's curiosity was satisfied by "pretty country." Fred did not envy man his newest chase. "Dream your fevered dreams!" he concluded.

In the quarter century since "Fred on Space" men have gone on dreaming about space and acting upon their dreams, with astonishing results. But in their treatments of space exploration in this period, as I have tried to show, our writers frequently revealed a caste of mind that Fred and his creator would find familiar. Now, with the successful entry of American space exploration into the era of the space shuttle, those literary treatments may well change. "The shuttle could make going into space so routine," Henry S. F. Cooper, Jr., has written, "that it would become an integral part of life on earth; indeed, if NASA has its way, things on earth may never be quite the same again." If NASA has its way, in other words, space flights may come to seem no more exotic than flights to Europe and, as Mailer hoped in *Of a Fire on the Moon*, men who speak like Shakespeare may regularly ride the rockets, returning with reports that draw us more and more toward the stars.

In a book following in the wake of the shuttle's success, *The High Road* (1981), Ben Bova energetically takes up NASA's case. He portrays another space race beyond that with the Russians: a race to save the earth. He paints a grim picture of coming global disaster and mass death; the end of civilization appears just around the corner. The only solution is to look to space and the opportunity it offers for creating a new and better society. With the shuttle we have the means to begin the task; we can send people into space to initiate the manufacturing and mineral extraction processes that eventually will lead to large numbers of people living in space. The issue, Bova maintains, is human survival—and space is the answer. "Lift up your faces," he exhorts his readers. "The Sun smiles upon you. The Moon beckons." Another post-shuttle book, *The Space Shuttle Operator's Manual* (1982), capitalizes on the theorectical availability of space flight to a larger range of people. No longer are space journeys restricted to a small group of rigorously trained ex-fighter pilots, the book suggests with at least a measure of seriousness; they are now within the range of possibility for you and me. Drawn from copious NASA technical literature, the trade paperback, edited by two curators of the National Air and Space Museum, boils down into 150 illustrated pages detailed instructions and checklists for a successful shuttle flight. "We'd always thought of the book," the editors told *Publishers Weekly*, "as what you'd find in the glove compartment if you bought a shuttle," and the manual's brief introduction wishes new astronauts a "rewarding and fascinating" flight.

Operating a space shuttle may belong in the realm of fancy, but a ride aboard a shuttle is not. NASA regularly receives applications from would-be civilian passengers in space, and it takes the applications seriously enough to respond to each one and maintain an applicant file. At this writing a NASA task force is considering such matters as when extra room will be available on shuttle flights and what kinds of people—journalists, artists, celebrities, ordinary people—might be invited on board. The *Wall Street Journal* reported that the task force is leaning toward passengers who can "communicate the experience" of space, which may mean that journalists and artists will receive special attention. It is clear, at any event, that extra seats will be available on shuttle orbiters beyond those needed for the astronaut crews—and clear as well that NASA means to fill them. "In the normal course of things," the task-force chairman told the *Journal*, "I'd expect several people to fly by the end of this decade, maybe a half-dozen or so starting in 1986 or 1987."*

But of course NASA might not have its way in its plans for the future. Despite the shuttle's success and the possibilities it offers for continued and expanded space exploration, there may be little effort in space in the immediate future—or little effort beyond that in service of military ends. The means for a new era of space exploration may be at hand, but the national will for a serious leap forward may be lacking. This paradoxical situation, in which technical capacity in space in the 1980s appears far in advance of the public mood, provides the conclusion for James Michener's ambitious novelistic treatment of American space exploration in *Space* (1982).

With the same historical sweep that marks his other popular novels, Michener takes on the entire space age, from the capture of German rocket scientists after the fall of Hitler to plans for a fourth shuttle flight, and he concludes the book with a checklist of activities in future space exploration, among them a mission to greet Halley's Comet, the installation of a space telescope, retrieval of rock samples from Mars and eventually a manned flight to the planet, and a permanent station in space. The plans are announced by Stanley Mott, a space scientist and

---

*Hortense Calisher's novel *Mysteries of Motion*, published in late 1983, drew on the possibility of the shuttle transporting ordinary people into space. Set near the end of our century, the story follows the shuttle flight of 100 people, including pregnant women and people with various infirmities, from polluted earth to "the first public habitat in space." Joyce Carol Oates, reviewing the novel, thought it made space travel "seem not at all visionary but merely practical, inevitable. Earth as the humanists would know it is finished."

NASA official, one of several figures whose careers Michener traces through the space program; Mott outlines his plans to a new Senator, the wife of the heroic astronaut John Pope, who is about to become a member of the Space Committee. Immediately Mott hears the familiar objections: the American people are not prepared to lavish more money on space; NASA should be placed in the Defense Department and serve only military needs; basic space research should be left to universities. Mott resists, fearing that if we back away from large-scale space exploration we will lose the momentum we have created and slip into second-class status in science and technology. But the last words on the subject are given to John Pope. He quotes a Korean journalist (a figure reminiscent of Oriana Fallaci) who in a book about American space exploration maintained that the flights to the moon were based on a sense of national challenge and that the country will not press forward again until it perceives a new challenge. Pope's wife, the new Senator, agrees: "We challenged the Moon, and Mars, Jupiter and Saturn, and we won. Now we must wait for the next great adventure."

Reluctantly, Michener seems to agree as well. Throughout the novel Mott's defense of space exploration as a quest for knowledge of the universe is sympathetically portrayed, as are the courageous and technically demanding space flights of Pope and a group of fellow astronauts known as the Solid Six. Michener's own sense of space flight seems summed up when near the end of the book Mott says: "When the mind of man ceases to thrust outward, it begins to contract and wither." If we fail to follow up with space exploration, he adds, we will repeat the error of Spain and Portugal in failing to pursue their fifteenth-century discoveries. "They allowed other nations to take up the joyous burden of developing new ideas, and from this decline they never recovered." Through Mott and the astronauts Michener portrays space exploration as a stirring adventure of the mind and spirit, a search for knowledge and an experience of awe. Space exploration may inform us about earth and cause us to cherish it all the more, but the focus in *Space* is on space more than earth—on the outward journey of minds and machines into the universe and its secrets.

Yet Mott believes that a national consensus in support of space exploration no longer exists. As a result, the period immediately ahead seems likely to be one of only modest accomplishments in space. To express the new mood, Michener creates a Dr. Leopold Strabismus, a charlatan who plays on fears of science and intellectual discovery and at the novel's end is leading a fundamentalist religious crusade that opposes further space exploration and inquiries into the origins of the universe. There is little to be done, Mott says, about Strabismus and regressive attitudes in the country he panders to except "bear with them. Admit that if society did not yearn for them, they wouldn't achieve the power they do. And hope that like Savonarola, they pass quickly without doing too much damage."

At the end of *Space*, space exploration is stalled, confronted with antiscience feelings and awaiting some new challenge to stir the populace. Nonetheless, the novel is an ardent celebration of the space age as a triumph of individual courage and national planning, technical skill and scientific curiosity. Like Allen Drury in *The Throne of Saturn*, Michener has done his research in the history of the space program and the technical details of space flights; indeed, for long stretches the book seems more a nonfiction account of the space program than a novel. And like Drury, Michener sets space events against a background of social and political developments in the country. The most dramatic (and fictional) part of the book is a flight to the dark side of the moon, *Apollo 18*, during which two astronauts are killed on the moon by a freak radiation storm and John Pope must pilot the spacecraft back to earth alone. During the return flight he appears on television and addresses the earth: "Mankind was born of

matter that accreted in space. We've seen dramatically
these past few days how things far off in space can affect us
deeply. We were meant to be in space, to wrestle with it, to
probe its secrets.'' Then Pope speaks to the wife of one of
the dead astronauts he has left behind: "I'd like especially
to say to Doris Linley that her husband was coming home
with a multitude of secrets and new theories, and we feel
his loss most grievously. The world will have to wait till
next time, Doris!" The comment captures Michener's
hope that space exploration will continue whatever the
costs and despite the flattened mood of the moment. What
is at stake in the flights to the stars is the mystery of life itself. To back away from that pursuit, his novel argues, is
to retreat from the very essence of the human adventure.

In the event that Michener's hope is realized (NASA
forging ahead, shuttle flights becoming routine, prophets
like Ben Bova correct in the space scenarios they construct,
those who can "communicate the experience" aboard the
orbiters) we may come to look back upon the preference of
E. B. White's Fred and others for "pretty country" rather
than the stars as simply a period of homesickness at the
start of a great journey. But even then, our destination de-
cisively outward, our deepest feelings may still turn inward; even though we fully commit ourselves to the stars,
the lure of home may remain with us, a tie we cannot
wholly sever. We may still find ourselves, as Loren Eiseley
believed, under the spell of a "greater and a green enchantment." The Russian poet Andrei Voznesensky offered the same thought in the closing lines of a poem
called "Earth":

> Somewhere on Mars
>   a visitor from Earth
> Will take out a handful of warm, brown earth
> And lovingly gaze at the blue-green sphere,
> Never distant,
> Ever near!

Writing in 1982 about the future of space exploration, Harrison Schmitt, who spent three days on the moon ten years earlier during the final Apollo flight, still recalled the sight from the lunar surface of the rising earth. He wrote: "That lonesome, marbled piece of blue with ancient seas and continental rafts will remain our home as we journey the solar system. The modern challenge, emphasized by our travels, is to both use and protect that home, together, as people of Earth. If we are successful the historians of the solar system, when some day they write of the people of Earth, may say that this was their greatest act."

A similar sense of earth as our inescapable home is at the center of Kenneth Brower's *The Starship and the Canoe* (1978), a journalistic report on the divergent lives of a father captured by the imagination of space and a son devoted to the revival of ancient adventure on earth. The father, Freeman Dyson, is an eminent mathematician and physicist and a leading proponent of space travel. Dyson has urged space travel not only for the purpose of scientific discovery but for the spiritual benefit of providing mankind with open frontiers. In the late 1950s he had joined with other scientists in developing an alternative to rocketry as a means of space travel. Dyson believed that the rockets that powered the Apollo flights were far too expensive for the purpose; space travel—as he argued in his book *Disturbing the Universe* (1979)—had to be cheap and broadly available before it could have a "liberating influence on human affairs." With his colleagues Dyson sought to construct a spaceship powered by the detonation of nuclear bombs that would allow scientists, including Dyson himself, to journey to the moon, Mars, and Saturn. Eventually the project lost out to NASA support of chemical rockets as the means for space ventures. In the 1970s Dyson's son, George, was living a subsistence existence along the coastline of British Columbia. He had constructed a house in a towering tree and traveled the complex waterways of the region in a home-made ocean-going canoe, actions which stemmed from a view of himself as one who, through example, was helping restore ecological sanity to an endangered world.

Brower moves his book back and forth between the sharply disparate views of father and son, recounting Freeman's theories on space travel and colonization, George's on returning to primitive Indian ways. The book ends with a guarded reunion of father and son, after years of estrangement, during a camping trip on a remote island. Brower also gives his own view of the lives of the two men: although Freeman's life is one of achievement and vision, it is George's life that he is most comfortable with. The earth seems to Brower, as it does to George, to offer sufficient room for adventure and exploration. Beyond this, there remains the endlesss process of rediscovery. Whereas Freeman finds the term "earthbound" limiting, Brower finds the word has a "snug and comfortable sound." Even if Freeman is right and human destiny ultimately is in the stars, Brower wants to believe that man will look back on the "youth of the race as the best time" since there seems to be little in space beyond astonishing sights to appeal to the senses. "I have a theory," he says, "that Columbus, Erickson, and Magellan, in their old age, remembered the sand of new beaches between their toes, the winds of new continents on their faces, the strange smells, the strange calls in the forest, as much as they remembered the sights. Our sensibilities evolved on Earth, and will be most rewarded there."

The division Brower locates in the lives of a father and son between the lure of earth and the attraction of the stars brings to mind the way Michael Collins concludes *Carrying the Fire*. He prints an address he gave to a joint session of Congress after the return of *Apollo 11* in which he recalled that during the moon flight the temperature of the spacecraft was controlled by a slow rotating motion. "As we turned," he explained, "the earth and the moon alternately appeared in our windows. We had our choice. We could look toward the moon, toward Mars, toward our future in space, toward the New Indies, or we could look back toward the earth, our home, with the problems spawned over more than a millennium of human occupancy." The choice Collins and his colleagues made was for both views. "We looked both ways. We saw both, and I think that is what our nation must do."

Our accounts of space exploration have looked both ways as well. But the look back at earth has seemed, for the time being at least, the most appealing, the most comforting, even the most stirring. "Pretty country" still claims us. As Robert Frost once remarked, outer space still "Stays more popu*lar/* Than popul*ous.*" Collins also relates that he now keeps in his livingroom a framed photograph showing a thin crescent against a black background. When people see it they invariably say, "Oh, the moon!" But it is a photograph of the earth.

References

Preface

Armstrong, Neil; Collins, Michael; Aldrin, Edwin E., Jr.
With Gene Farmer and Dora Jane Hamblin. *First on the
Moon: A Voyage with Neil Armstrong, Michael Collins,
and Edwin E. Aldrin, Jr.* Boston: Little, Brown, 1970.
"Armstrong Recalls Historic Walk and Sight of a Planet Left
Behind." *New York Times*, 20 July 1979, p. 12.
Lewis, Richard S. *The Voyages of Apollo: The Exploration
of the Moon.* New York: Quadrangle, 1974.
McDougall, Walter A. "Technology and Statecraft in the
Space Age—Toward the History of a Saltation." *American Historical Review*, October 1982, pp. 1010-1040.
Mumford, Lewis. *The Myth of the Machine: The Pentagon
of Power.* New York: Harcourt Brace Jovanovich, 1970.
"Reconnaissance of the Moon." *New York Times*, 25 December 1968, p. 30.
Seelye, John. *Prophetic Waters.* New York: Oxford University Press, 1977.

Chapter 1: Great-Circle Sailing

Aldrin, Edwin E., Jr. With Wayne Warga. *Return to Earth.*
New York: Random House, 1973.
Arlen, Michael J. "The Space Race." *The New Yorker*, 22
September 1962, p. 37.
Bellow, Saul. *Mr. Sammler's Planet.* New York: Viking,
1970.

Berry, Wendell. "The Debate Sharpens." In *Space Colonies*. Edited by Stewart Brand. New York: Penguin Books, 1977.

Boorstin, Daniel. *Democracy and Its Discontents*. New York: Random House, 1974.

Bradbury, Ray. In *10:56:20 PM/EDT/7/20/69: The Historic Conquest of the Moon as Reported to the American People by CBS News Over the CBS Television Network*. New York: CBS, 1970.

———. In *Why Man Explores*. Washington, D.C.: Government Printing Office, 1977.

Brautigan, Richard. "Comments on O'Neill's Space Colonies." In *Space Colonies*. Edited by Stewart Brand. New York: Penguin Books, 1977.

Cousins, Norman. In *Why Man Explores*. Washington, D. C.: Government Printing Office, 1977.

Cronin, Vincent. *The View from Planet Earth*. New York: Morrow, 1981.

Dos Passos, John. "On the Way to the Moon Shot." *National Review*, 9 February 1971, pp. 135-136.

Dubos, René. *A God Within*. New York: Scribner's, 1972.

Dyson, Freeman. *Disturbing the Universe*. New York: Harper & Row, 1979.

Eliot, T. S. *The Complete Poems, 1909-1950*. New York: Harcourt Brace, 1952.

Emerson, Ralph Waldo. *The Complete Essays and Other Writings*. Edited by Brooks Atkinson. New York: Modern Library, 1940.

Engdahl, Sylvia. *Our World is Enough*. New York: Atheneum, 1979.

Ferkiss, Victor. *Technological Man*. New York: Braziller, 1969.

Kesey, Ken. "Comments on O'Neill's Space Colonies." In *Space Colonies*. Edited by Stewart Brand. New York: Penguin Books, 1977.

Leonard, John. "Science, Virtuous Villain." *New York Times Book Review*, 9 April 1978, p. 3.

Marx, Leo. *The Machine in the Garden*. New York: Oxford University Press, 1964.

_____. "The Impact of the Railroad on the American Imagination, as a Possible Comparison for the Space Impact." In *The Railroad and the Space Program: An Exploration in Historical Analogy*. Edited by Bruce Mazlish. Cambridge, Mass.: M.I.T. Press, 1965.

_____. "American Literary Culture and the Fatalistic View of Technology." *Alternative Futures*, Spring 1980, pp. 45-70.

Mazlish, Bruce. "Historical Analogy: The Railroad and the Space Program and Their Impact on Society." In *The Railroad and the Space Program: An Exploration in Historical Analogy*. Edited by Bruce Mazlish. Cambridge, Mass.: M.I.T. Press, 1965.

_____. "Following the Sun." *The Wilson Quarterly*, Autumn 1980, pp. 90-93.

McDowell, Edwin. "Can Man Turn His Back on Space?" *Wall Street Journal*, 21 April 1972, p. 8.

McWhirter, William A. "Tom Benton at Eighty." *Life*, October 3, 1969, pp. 64-70.

Michener, James. In *Apollo: Ten Years Since Tranquillity Base*. Edited by Richard P. Hallion and Tom D. Crouch. Washington, D.C.: National Air and Space Museum, 1979.

Oberg, James E. *Red Star in Orbit*. New York: Random House, 1981.

Powers, J. F. *Look How the Fish Live*. New York: Knopf, 1975.

Sagan, Carl. *Murmurs of Earth*. New York: Random House, 1978.

_____. *Broca's Brain*. New York: Random House, 1979.

_____. *Cosmos*. New York: Random House, 1980.

Schmitt, Harrison. "The New Ocean of Space." *Sky and Telescope*, October 1982, pp. 327-329.

Slater, Philip. *Earthwalk*. Garden City, N.Y.: Doubleday, 1974.

Snow, C. P. *The Two Cultures and the Scientific Revolution.* New York: Cambridge University Press, 1959.

————. "One Man's Universe." *New York Times Book Review,* 24 April 1977, p. 10.

Thoreau, Henry David. *Walden and Other Writings.* Edited by Brooks Atkinson. New York: Modern Library, 1937.

Tomkins, Calvin. *Off the Wall.* Garden City, N.Y.: Doubleday, 1980.

Von Braun, Wernher. "A Step Toward Immortality." In *Moon: Man's Greatest Adventure.* Edited by Davis Thomas. New York: Abrams, 1970.

Whitmer, Peter O. "Ken Kesey's Search for the American Frontier." *Saturday Review,* May-June 1983, pp. 23-27.

Wilford, John Noble. "Last Apollo Wednesday; Scholars Assess Program." *New York Times,* 3 December 1972, p. 1.

Williams, Raymond. *Marxism and Literature.* Oxford: Oxford University Press, 1977.

Wolfe, Tom. Foreword to *Nine Lies About America*, by Arnold Beichman. New York: Library Press, 1972.

————. "Columbus and the Moon." *New York Times,* 20 July 1979, p. 25.

Chapter 2: The Last Miracle

Auden, W. H. *Collected Poems.* New York: Random House, 1976.

Arendt, Hannah. *The Human Condition.* Chicago: University of Chicago Press, 1958.

————. "Man's Conquest of Space." *American Scholar,* Autumn 1963, pp. 527-540.

Barrett, William. *Time of Need.* New York: Harper & Row, 1972.

Bauer, Raymond A. *Second-Order Consequences: A Methodological Essay on the Impact of Technology.* Cambridge, Mass.: M.I.T. Press, 1969.

Diamond, Edwin. *The Rise and Fall of the Space Age.* Garden City, N.Y.: Doubleday, 1964.

Eiseley, Loren. *The Invisible Pyramid*. New York: Scribner's, 1970.

Etzioni, Amitai. *The Moon-Doggle*. Garden City, N.Y.: Doubleday, 1964.

Fairlie, Henry. "By Jupiter!" *New Republic*, 7 April 1979, pp. 18-21.

Jackson, Barbara [Ward]. *Spaceship Earth*. New York: Columbia University Press, 1966.

Kennedy, Eugene. "Earthrise: The Dawning of a New Spiritual Awareness." *New York Times Magazine*, 15 April 1979, p. 14.

Marty, Martin. "A Humanist's View of Space Research." *Chicago Today*, Autumn 1966, pp. 26-33.

Mazlish, Bruce. "The Idea of Progress." *Daedalus*, Summer 1963, pp. 447-461.

Moravia, Alberto. "Reflections on the Moon." *McCall's*, January 1970, p. 43.

Mumford, Lewis. *The Myth of the Machine: The Pentagon of Power*. New York: Harcourt Brace Jovanovich, 1970.

Noel, Daniel C. "Re-Entry: Earth Images in Post-Apollo Culture." *Michigan Quarterly Review*, Spring 1979, pp. 155-176.

"Roads to Hell—or Heaven." *New York Times*, 7 October 1957, p. 26.

"Stride Into Space." *New York Times*, 6 October 1957, p. 10 E.

Thompson, William Irwin. *Passages About Earth*. New York: Harper & Row, 1974.

Tillich, Paul. *The Future of Religions*. Edited by Jerald C. Brauer. New York: Harper & Row, 1966.

Updike, John. *Rabbit, Run*. New York: Knopf, 1960.

————. *Rabbit is Rich*. New York: Knopf, 1981.

Chapter 3: Just People

Aldrin, Edwin E., Jr. With Wayne Warga. *Return to Earth*. New York: Random House, 1973.

Collins, Michael. *Carrying the Fire*. New York: Farrar,

Straus and Giroux, 1974.

"Cosmonaut diary tells of loneliness." *Chicago Tribune*, 16 August 1983, p. 5.

Cunningham, Walter. With Mickey Herskowitz. *The All-American Boys*. New York: Macmillan, 1977.

Davis, Maggie. *Eagles*. New York: Morrow, 1980.

Friedman, Bruce Jay. *About Harry Towns*. New York: Knopf, 1974.

Greene, Daniel St. Albin. "What Next After You've Walked on the Moon?" *National Observer*, 17 May 1975, p. 1.

Grissom, Betty and Still, Henry. *Starfall*. New York: Crowell, 1974.

Grissom, Virgil. *Gemini!* New York: Macmillan, 1968.

Irwin, James B. With William A. Emerson, Jr. *To Rule the Night*. Philadelphia: Holman, 1973.

Magee, John. "High Flight." In *Carrying the Fire*. By Michael Collins. New York: Farrar, Straus and Giroux, 1974.

Mailer, Norman. *Of a Fire on the Moon*. Boston: Little, Brown, 1970.

O'Leary, Brian. *The Making of an Ex-Astronaut*. New York: Houghton Mifflin, 1970.

Rhodes, Richard. *Sons of Earth*. New York: Coward, McCann & Geoghegan, 1981.

Zweig, Paul. *The Adventurer*. New York: Basic Books, 1974.

Chapter 4: A Meaning to Us

Auden, W. H. *Collected Poems*. New York: Random House, 1976.

Bellow, Saul. *Mr. Sammler's Planet*. New York: Viking, 1970.

Blumgarten, James. *The Astronaut*. New York: Warner Books, 1974.

Caidin, Martin. *The Cape*. Garden City, N.Y.: Doubleday, 1971.

Cronin, Vincent. *The View from Planet Earth*. New York: Morrow, 1981.

Drury, Allen. *The Throne of Saturn*. Garden City, N.Y.: Doubleday, 1971.

Field, Edward. "After the Moon Walk." *New York Review of Books*, 18 July 1974, p. 15.

Honan, William E. "Le Mot Juste for the Moon." *Esquire*, July 1969, p. 55.

Lindbergh, Anne Morrow. *Earth Shine*. New York: Harcourt, Brace & World, 1969.

Lipsyte, Robert. *Liberty Two*. New York: Simon & Schuster, 1974.

MacLeish, Archibald. "Voyage to the Moon." In *Moonstruck: An Anthology of Lunar Poetry*. Edited by Robert Phillips. New York: Vanguard, 1974.

————. *Riders on the Earth*. Boston: Houghton Mifflin, 1978.

Mailer, Norman. *Of a Fire on the Moon*. Boston: Little, Brown, 1970.

Morris, Wright. *A Bill of Rites, A Bill of Wrongs, A Bill of Goods*. New York: New American Library, 1968.

————. *The Fork River Space Project*. New York: Harper & Row, 1977.

Stupple, James, "A Literature Against the Future." *American Scholar*, Spring 1977, pp. 215-220.

Updike, John. *Rabbit Redux*. New York: Knopf, 1971.

Vonnegut, Kurt, Jr. "The Manned Missiles." In *The Norton Anthology of Short Fiction*. Edited by R. V. Cassill. New York: Norton, 1978.

Chapter 5: Lots of Rocks

Boyle, Charles P. *Space Among Us: Some Effects of Space Research on Society*. Washington, D.C.: Aerospace Industries Association, 1974.

Dickey, James. "The Triumph of Apollo 7." *Life*, November 1, 1968, p. 26.

————. *Sorties*. Garden City, N.Y.: Doubleday, 1971.

————. *The Strength of Fields.* Garden City, N.Y.: Doubleday, 1979.

Frost, Robert. *The Poetry of Robert Frost.* Edited by Edward Connery Lathem. New York: Holt, Rinehart and Winston, 1969.

Goldstein, Laurence. " 'The End of All Our Exploring': The Moon Landing and Modern Poetry." *Michigan Quarterly Review*, Spring 1979, pp. 318-342.

Phillips, Robert, ed. *Moonstruck: An Anthology of Lunar Poetry.* New York: Vanguard, 1974.

Rich, Adrienne. *A Wild Patience Has Taken Me This Far.* New York: Norton, 1981.

Updike, John. "The Moons of Jupiter." *American Scholar*, Autumn 1982, pp. 483-486.

Vale, Charles, ed. *The Spirit of St. Louis.* New York: Doran, 1927.

Vas Dias, Robert, ed. *Inside Outer Space.* New York: Anchor Books, 1970.

Vonnegut, Kurt, Jr. *Between Time and Timbuktu.* New York: Delacorte, 1972.

Worden, Alfred M. *Hello Earth.* Los Angeles: Nash, 1974.

Chapter 6: Visit Earth

Cooper, Henry S. F., Jr. *Apollo on the Moon.* New York: Dial, 1969.

————. *Moon Rocks.* New York: Dial, 1970.

————. *Thirteen: The Flight That Failed.* New York: Dial, 1973.

————. *A House in Space.* New York: Holt, Rinehart and Winston, 1976.

————. *The Search for Life on Mars.* New York: Holt, Rinehart and Winston, 1980.

Fallaci, Oriana. *If the Sun Dies.* New York: Atheneum, 1966.

Held, George. "Men on the Moon: American Novelists Explore Lunar Space." *Michigan Quarterly Review*, Spring 1979, pp. 318-342.

Kramer, Hilton. "Aquarius takes an ego-trip to the moon." *Chicago Tribune Book World*, 10 January 1971, p. 1.

Mailer, Norman. *Of a Fire on the Moon.* Boston: Little, Brown, 1970.

Poirier, Richard. *Norman Mailer.* New York: Viking, 1972.

Werge, Thomas. "An Apocalyptic Voyage: God, Satan, and the American Tradition in Norman Mailer's *Of a Fire on the Moon.*" In *America in Change.* Edited by Ronald Weber. Notre Dame, Ind.: University of Notre Dame Press, 1972.

Wolfe, Tom. *The Right Stuff.* New York: Farrar, Straus and Giroux, 1979.

Chapter 7: Pretty Country

Blooston, George. "Always Wanted to Fly the Space Shuttle?" *Publishers Weekly*, 18 June 1982, pp. 44-46.

Bova, Ben. *The High Road.* Boston: Houghton Mifflin, 1981.

Brower, Kenneth. *The Starship and the Canoe.* New York: Holt, Rinehart and Winston, 1978.

Calisher, Hortense. *Mysteries of Motion.* New York: Doubleday, 1983.

Collins, Michael. *Carrying the Fire.* New York: Farrar, Straus and Giroux, 1974.

Cooper, Henry S. F., Jr. "A Reporter at Large." *The New Yorker*, 9 February 1981, pp. 43-105.

Dyson, Freeman. *Disturbing the Universe.* New York: Harper & Row, 1979.

Eiseley, Loren. *The Invisible Pyramid.* New York: Scribner's, 1970.

Frost, Robert. *The Poetry of Robert Frost.* Edited by Edward Connery Lathem. New York: Holt, Rinehart and Winston, 1969.

Joels, Kerry Mark and Kennedy, Gregory P. *The Space Shuttle Operator's Manual.* New York: Ballantine

Books, 1982.

Large, Arlen J. " 'Dear NASA,' They Write, 'Won't You Take Me Along?' " *Wall Street Journal*, 25 April 1983, p. 1.

Michener, James. *Space*. New York: Random House, 1982.

Oates, Joyce Carol. "The Citizen Courier in Outer Space." *New York Times Book Review*, 6 November 1983, p. 7.

Voznesensky, Andrei. "Earth." In *Soviet Russian Poetry of the 1950s-1970s*. Moscow: Progress Publishers, 1981.

White, E. B. "Fred on Space." *The New Yorker*, 16 November 1957, pp. 46-47.

Index